What people are _ _ _ _ _ _
and *The Palace...*

"I have known Jonathan Seiver for many years and have great respect for his heart for God, his scholarship, and his integrity. Jonathan has written *The Palace.* I recommend *The Palace,* and I recommend Jonathan."

—Randy Clark, D. Min., Th. D.
Overseer of the Apostolic Network of Global Awakening

"Too profound and dense to come from the natural, these visions given to Jonathan Seiver will connect with something deep inside you that you thought lost and provide revelation enough to close any imagined distance between you and your Heavenly Father. The glimpses of the King in these pages will set your heart on fire and bring an increase of your hunger for intimacy with Him. Furthermore, these visions carry a dramatic release from guilt and shame and a newfound sense of freedom to operate with authority in pursuit of bringing the Kingdom to Earth."

—Braden Heckman
CEO, WP Films

Having known Jonathan for several years, I have always been impressed with the purity of his heart and also with his pursuit of the heart of God. I have been blessed to see that he has steadily remained in that pursuit in seasons of victory and seasons of struggle. After reading his book, I feel even more blessed to have been able to share in his experiences through this series of visions. *The Palace* has a beautiful mix of vision and personal experience written in such a way as to edify the whole body of Christ. Although he says the book is not written as an in-depth theological study, it certainly has sound theological influence throughout. While not lacking in depth, it is written in a very simple and easy-to-receive way. As I read, I was taken into these vivid encounters and could clearly see what Jonathan described.

Our work in Brazil is primarily with women and children living in abuse and the sex trades. I cried as I read this book because these beautiful perspectives of the Father and of the way the Father sees us are exactly what our precious ones on the streets are needing. I intend to share parts of these visions as we work in our discipleship groups with our women. Whether you are just beginning your journey with the Father or have been walking with him for many years, I am sure that you will be blessed and edified by *The Palace*.

—Nic Billman
Founder and Director, Shores of Grace Ministries
Recife, Brazil

THE PALACE

*A Prophetic Journey through the Cultures of This
Age and The Kingdom of the Age to Come*

Jonathan Seiver

ISBN-13:9781517048259

ISBN-10:1517048257

Library of Congress Control Number: 2015913966
CreateSpace Independent Publishing Platform
North Charleston, South Carolina

DEDICATION

To my Dad and Mom:
Who brought me to places and
modeled for me a lifestyle
that made this book possible.

ACKNOWLEDGMENTS

Thank you to all who helped with various aspects of this book throughout the journey: Curt Malloy, Aaron Nickerson, Mary Hasz, Dennis Melnichuk, Ryan Bundra, Jeremy Seiver, Cameron Ringer, Jobe Ringer, Audrey Ringer, Fyne Ashmore, Susan Jomantas, Rachel Beanblossom, Carolyn Smith, and Alexis Smith—I appreciate all your help! To Tara Browder for your extensive grammatical editing and acquaintanceship. To Nick Bundra for your adroit lexical savvy and deft linguistic mastery. Thanks also to those who offered cultural insights on various chapters: Heather Sheu, Scott Ma, Matt Lee, Rihanna Teixeira, and Shana Abreu.

A special shout out to Brenda Peters who told me ahead of time that this book was going to happen and what format it would take.

I might have been able to complete this book without all of you, but it would have been a much longer and difficult journey! Love to you all.

CHAPTER LIST

FOREWORD

My wife, Brenda, and I have known Jonathan for a dozen years or more. He has been an amazing spiritual son to us. For several years, Jonathan administrated our Mozambique missions team for us and did an excellent job. We spent many hours discussing the things of the Kingdom and prophetic words and insights about his future and the future of the church. We had both given him prophetic words, recorded on cassette tapes, before we knew who he was. He listened to those tapes frequently, praying about every prophetic statement and asking God for confirmation and application.

As an author of more than twenty Christian books, I look for a number of things when I read someone else's books. I want a book that has plenty of elements of divine revelation, creativity, and surprise. I want it to keep enticing me to read more. I'm looking for something on every page to keep me interested. I'm not looking for repetitive preaching and things I've read or heard many times before.

Jonathan's book has it all, but in a different and unique way. He doesn't use a lot of tease elements or mysterious clues as to what's coming next. You just want to know what's coming next because what you've already read touched your heart, and you could identify so well with it and all the allegorical applications.

The Palace is not just another religious book to teach us how to live a good and successful life—one that will bless us down here and get us safely to Heaven as well. This adventure into the heart of the King of kings has all the depth of such classics as John Bunyan's *Pilgrim's Progress* and the more recent *The Final Quest* by Rick Joyner.

Based on visions received in times of intimacy with God, Jonathan Seiver shares without hype or embellishment the adventures available to every Christian who deeply desires to know and walk with God. It truly is a book which describes his own journey, but it also has so many nuggets of truth that will enrich every sincere reader. It is my opinion that reading this book once is not enough. Too many valuable gems will be lost and forgotten with just one reading. It would make an excellent devotional to be read through several times in one year.

This book addresses several weaknesses in the Western church today. First of all, there has been a great lack of passion to know God intimately with the majority of Christians. Focusing on the Palace of the King is not their top priority. In the beginning of Jonathan's story, not many knew too much about the Palace, and very few were willing to drop what they were doing to find out. Fortunately, the Holy Spirit is certainly refocusing the church on intimacy and Kingdom priorities today.

Other weaknesses addressed are the tendencies for human pride and the flesh to compete for selfish ambition and to ignore the needs of others. The lack of unity and willingness to sacrifice for others and our King comes through loud and clear. But with every revealed weakness, the King is there to show the reader a better way to live.

I loved the chapters which address the special needs of various people groups, including ethnic groups and women. God downloaded some very special and insightful concepts that we would do well to apply.

But the most important element of this book, by far, is the revelation that the King is waiting for every one of His subjects to come spend time with Him and learn from Him. He has time for each one and will equip and train us for the inescapable battles we will face, for powerful and effective evangelism, and for loving relationships.

Finally, let me say again that this book is the real deal, and Jonathan Seiver has paid a price for the revelation he has revealed in this book. I know of no young man of God who has kept such a pure heart and gentle spirit, while facing some of the toughest trials a young man can go through. I trust his prophetic journey, described in this book, will be as great a blessing as knowing him has been to Brenda and me.

Ben R. Peters
Author, International Conference Speaker,
Co-Founder of Open Heart Ministries and Kingdom Sending Center

INTRODUCTION

The following is a series of visions that are very dear to my heart. At times, these experiences with God touched me in such a profound way that I found them difficult to convey in words. They shaped both the way I view God and myself. I initially assumed these visions were fashioned by God to simply encourage me during a season when I was crying out for more of him. Because the initial visions were very personal in nature, this assumption was reinforced. However, it soon became evident that God was giving these revelations and experiences not only for my benefit but also for the benefit of others.

The king and I are the main characters in the vision. Occasionally, I was an observer, usually with the king as the events took place. However, most of the story proceeded with me actively involved in the vision. Throughout this experience, my personality in real life was blended with my personality in the vision, but they are one and the same for the most part. For example, when I make comments like "I *used* to think..." or "I always *wondered*...," I am referring to both previous thoughts I had in the vision as well as mindsets I previously held in reality.

The setting and feel of the initial vision was similar to the beginning of the Disney movie *Aladdin*, only more realistic and less Middle Eastern. While the book's cover properly communicates the concept of a boy allured by a palace, the palace in the vision is more accurately depicted by the descriptions and details provided throughout the book. My intent is that you will be able to both envision the scenes portrayed and experience the emotions conveyed along this prophetic journey.

Each vision lasted between ten and twenty minutes. I received them while awake with my physical eyes closed but my spiritual eyes wide open. When I began to see a new vision, I would immediately experience the same emotions and the history of the previous visions. Even if several months had passed since my last one, I immediately found myself right where I left off in the previous vision. After each vision ended, I described to the best of my ability in writing all that I had just watched, felt, and experienced.

The visions did not always unfold as I expected or, sometimes even, desired. At times, my natural mind would be thinking, "I would never actually do what I'm doing right now." This was especially true in the chapters *Ebony* and *The Last Battle.* At other times, I would be thinking, "I'm not sure if what I'm seeing is even correct." However, I innately knew that I needed to let the visions ensue as God directed. The moment I tried to force myself to see something based on my own logic and reasoning would have been the moment that these experiences would have been emptied of their power. God desired the freedom to convey what he wanted without the interference of my logic, and, later, I saw that every principle he revealed to me in these visions is found in the Bible.

Several sociocultural and ethnic groups appear in the story. As with any people group, the factors leading to present trends and dynamics within sociocultural and ethnic groups are as diverse as the people groups themselves. Several key themes and messages for various peoples exist within this story. Just as Jesus' parables often reduced complex situations into a very basic story in order to highlight a certain lesson, so this story is often parabolic in nature for the sake of conveying specific truths. These sections should be seen as simplifying a matter to a few core components rather than overgeneralizing.

After some debate, I chose to include endnotes at the end of the book. This allowed me to further explain what I felt at certain times in the story. Occasionally, I used the endnotes to mention examples from the Bible that support the message of a particular scene. I hope the fact that I neither included lengthy explanations nor spoon-fed interpretations testifies to my desire for readers to not simply depend on my own personal experience and reasoning in order to understand the messages in this book. More important than my thoughts and reflections on the vision is the message that the king invites all of us to the palace to have our own unique, personal encounters with him.

This book is not an in-depth theological treatise. It is not meant to provide a complete discussion on every major spiritual topic. Additionally, because the story is a series of visions, the plot does not unfold with the typical suspense and character development of a modern-day novel. It is, instead, a collection of simple yet important messages illustrated through a prophetic journey. In light of this, my hope is that by the end of this book you will have a greater understanding of God and a deeper appreciation of his heart for you and others.

1

THE JOURNEY BEGINS

For as long as I can remember, I was an orphan. Despite the typical assumptions about orphans, I never really felt lonely or sorry for myself. When you've never known anything different, you don't think about what could have been. And my life wasn't that bad. I didn't have many possessions, of course, but I had what I needed. I survived.

Discontentment didn't lead me to search for the palace that day. Being older now, I've heard the critics' characterizations of those who seek out the palace—people at the end of their rope have no other options, so they look for the palace. The depressed, broken, or suicidal become so desperate that they set off on the journey after years of struggle. However, none of these problems were the catalyst for embarking on my journey to the palace. What was my motivation? Simply put, I was curious, and I had nothing to lose.

I didn't know much about the palace when I set out on my quest. I didn't even know much about myself for that matter. After all, how much self-awareness can a young child really possess? I must have been seven or eight at the time. Street orphans don't have parents to tell them their age or to preserve birth certificates from which to calculate their age. Instead, we do our best to compare ourselves physically with other children and try to guess our age accordingly.

I heard stories about the palace from people on the streets. Everyone wanted to give their two cents, but they didn't know much more than that. Their descriptions of the palace were mostly obscure, and each person's concept of the palace seemed to be patterned after what they hoped it to be. For example, if they hoped the palace was a welcoming place, then they would describe it to strangers as welcoming. If they wished it was fun, they would describe the palace as filled with entertaining activities.

"Somewhere in the kingdom there is a palace," some of the housewives in the alley told me as I departed.

"We don't know where it is, but we know it's out there," others added.

People also assured me that there was a king who lived there. But, again, no one knew much about him or how he spent his time.

"But he is good," most people affirmed, "just a little distant." Some of the old men on the street took a more philosophical approach, attempting to determine through reason whether or not the king actually ruled over a kingdom or not. In between chess games and coffee, they debated for hours without anyone ever coming to any conclusions. I'm not sure they even wanted to win; they just seemed to like to debate. The debate made them feel comfortable with their response, or lack of response, to the existence of the king. Even if they later changed their minds, as long as they could successfully defend their point of view on the palace or the king, they felt secure.

I was never into sitting around and listening to the old men argue. A few of the other kids were, and I discerned that this set them on a trajectory to become old, cantankerous men themselves. It seemed like a waste of time to argue if no one actually intended to find any real answers. "Maybe," I pondered to myself, "the king is not like the kings of old who ruled supremely but more like some kings of today who are honored and celebrated despite lacking any real or concrete authority over their kingdom." Answering my own pondering, I reasoned, "There's only one way to find out."

To be honest, the palace intrigued me more than the king did. I thought it would be nice to meet the king, but who knew if he would actually want to talk to me? To my knowledge, he had never taken the time to pay a visit to anyone in my town. Why would he suddenly be interested in me?

When people on the street learned of my quest—not that I knew many people to begin with—most thought I was wasting my time. People were okay with talking about the palace, but, if I mentioned that I actually wanted to visit it, they seemed to become agitated. Some of the older women, however, thought it was cute. As I passed by, they chatted among themselves, "Isn't that sweet? He's in a stage that every kid goes through. Let him have his fun."

So, with nothing to lose and a glimmer of hope of something to gain, I set out that day. As I journeyed through various streets and neighborhoods, I received little assistance on how to get to the palace. Some were utterly convinced they knew the way, but they excused themselves from providing directions by stating, "I just can't put it into words." Others said to go here or go there, but it was pretty clear they didn't know what they were talking about. Despite the lack of knowledge, the modus operandi of the village seemed to be, "If a kid asks me about the king, even though I have no idea, I have to give him an answer because I'm an adult." Since I wasn't interested in theoretical road maps to the king, I refused to spend much time talking with the people along the way.

As I passed through village after village, I realized a fascinating phenomenon. While everyone's view on the palace differed and few had interest in finding it, everyone knew how to get there if they really wanted to consider the matter. Even those who were most adamant about the palace not existing hinted through something in their voices that they really knew what it was and where it was. Because of all of the confusing instructions I received in my village, this surprised me. From my limited seven- or eight-year-old perspective, people knew more than they were willing to admit, and maybe even knew more than they wanted to know. Thus, without help from the folks who knew a lot and not much all at the same time, I simply followed the voice in the back of my mind saying, "Keep going this way."

After several days with few obstacles and no major excitement, I arrived at the palace. It appeared nice enough but not overly ornate like some of the palaces described in fairy tales. It was clearly well kept and had no signs of decay. I passed through a gateway and beheld a very wide set of about twenty steps, which lined almost the entire side of the palace. The stone steps led up to a series of pillars and then a large entrance. "So the palace really does exist!" I thought to myself, surprised yet not overly surprised.

Naturally, I was curious about going inside, but, without knowing the rules, I was unsure if I—or anyone else for that matter—was allowed inside. I wondered if the palace was like a museum with visiting hours where everyone who wanted could enter as long as they followed certain guidelines. I also considered the possibility that the king could get upset with me if he discovered me snooping around. I didn't want to ruin my first opportunity to meet the king or visit the palace.

What if this was all there was to the palace? What if I only got to look at it, admire it, and go home? This would explain why no one along the way seemed too excited about my going to the palace. Surely, if the palace was as great as I had hoped, many others would have come by now.

I wasn't sure what to do at this point, but, since no guards came after me, I just stood staring at the palace while wondering, "Is this all there is to this adventure?" This question was answered when I saw the king appear in the entryway of the palace and come down the steps toward me.

The king had a grandeur about him, but he didn't carry himself with the typical self-aggrandizing showiness that some might expect from a king. He walked with confidence and purpose yet not in a manner of trying to attract attention to himself. The king was not looking for people to grovel at his feet to satisfy his insecurity as some in authority do. He didn't carry himself with a lot of pomp. He didn't have to. He was completely secure. He did have a nice robe but not anything excessive. Rather, his grandeur stemmed from his genuine and resolute nature. He wasn't searching for flattery, putting on fronts, or trying to prove anything.

Despite the fact that I was a street kid with nothing to offer him, he approached me, asked me about my past, and listened to my story. I shared with him the typical day of a life on the streets. I had no idea why he would be interested in my life, but, nevertheless, on and on we spoke. He described various aspects of the palace and what took place there. In turn, I told him about my family, or lack thereof, the streets, and stealing and scavenging to survive. As I shared with him, I had a peculiar sense that he already knew the details of my life, but, since he kept asking questions, I kept answering them.

Discussions like these with the king occurred for many days. Each day, I arrived at the palace steps, the king met me, and we talked for a few hours. At night, I slept outside the walls around the palace courtyard. The guards didn't mind, and neither did I. After all, I was used to sleeping on the streets.

My relationship with the king was not a typical one. Talking to him was not like talking with others. It was not like being excited about meeting someone for the first time only for the novelty to soon dissipate. I never wearied of spending time with the king and never ceased to look forward to him descending the steps to meet with me. Unlike some old men who bore listeners by repeating the same stories, he captivated me every day with fresh stories of new aspects and dimensions of the kingdom. Each morning, I awoke with increasing expectation for my daily encounter with the king, and, every night, I would play our conversation through my mind, committing to memory what I could. Naturally, I got to know him better with each discussion and could almost consider him a friend. However, I still realized that I was a street kid and that he was a king.

Yet I had a deep hunger to know him more. For all of his sharing and self-disclosure, he was still a mystery to me. Why was he interested in me in the first place? Why was he choosing to spend time with me day after day? What did he gain from these encounters? How long would it be until he wearied of me? No matter the direction our interaction would take, I desired to understand the king and what made him and his kingdom tick. I longed to understand the kingdom more than anyone else ever had, and I still had plenty of questions. Somehow, I knew the answers lay inside the palace.

The opportunity to get some answers presented itself sooner than I expected in the form of a question from the king.

"Do you want to be my son?" he asked me one day.

I had never expected this. I had no grid for being anyone's son, let alone the king's.[1] Questions deluged my mind: "Do kings adopt sons?" "What would it be like to finally have a parent?" and "Why *me?*" My mind still submerged in these questions, I accepted his offer and took his hand as he led me up the staircase.

"So, the orphan boy from the streets will become the son of the king," I thought to myself. "Incredible!" I would no longer be a wanderer aimlessly roaming. I would finally belong.

2

ENTERING THE PALACE

As every adopted orphan will tell you, there's an indescribable joy that comes with finally being chosen. It's not just about having someone to provide for you or even about finally having parents. The greatest fulfillment is finally belonging. Not just belonging but belonging *to someone*. However, I was not focused at the moment on a life of being cared for and loved by a parent; I was thinking what any young boy in my place would be thinking, "Sweet! I finally get to see what's inside the palace!"

We ascended the steps for the first time together and entered through the large door at the top. This was the same one the king had exited through each day to meet me. The opening hallway was lined on both sides with tall, glass display cases. Each case was filled with old weapons and artifacts that were used in great battles of the past. I saw swords, helmets, shields, boots, and other materials used for warfare. Behind each artifact was a placard describing the object, its function, and the time period or battle in which it was used. The placards also revealed how each object had been wielded at a critical moment in history and thus brought about a great deliverance. I understood how swords, battleaxes, and other traditional weapons could be essential to victory. However, I didn't see, as the placards declared, how an entire battle could hinge on a helmet, shield, or metal boot covers.[2]

But, apparently, even the most unlikely of weapons could change history if utilized at the precise moment the king directed.

This "War Room," as I called it, fascinated me. Day after day, the king described his army's greatest victories. After hours of stories, I wanted to hear them all over again. When the king tells a story, it never gets old. It's one thing to hear a war story; it's quite another thing to hear it from the general who devised and carried out the decisive victory.

As the king spoke with me each day, an emerging desire arose in me to be like one of those fearless leaders from the past who fought valiantly with the army of the king. The king surprised me, however, by mentioning that many of the warriors were actually very hesitant and even timid when entering the battle.

"Yet," he added, "each one specifically followed my blueprint for success for the particular battle and, as a result, overcame."

This was reassuring since I assumed I would be terrified if I was ever required to go into a battle.

"Who knows?" I thought to myself. "Maybe I could be a great warrior some day!"

I didn't spend much time daydreaming because military commanders send trained soldiers to fight, not kids recently off the streets. I was young, but I at least understood enough to know that every child has far-fetched dreams that never materialize. Knowing that my chances at future military heroics were doubtful at best, I still had fun imagining them.

During the countless days in the War Room hearing tales of epic battles, I started to notice that the king seemed to desire to show me other places in the palace. I wasn't very interested in exploring other parts of the palace yet. For a boy, what could possibly be better than hearing about the great wars of the past? Despite his attempts to show me other places, I succeeded in convincing him to keep bringing me to my favorite corridor.

After many days of this, the king spoke to me in a firm but loving voice, "Son, I have much to show you." I could see in his eyes that he was saying, "It's not always in your best interest to get your own way!" I hadn't really thought about the king having an agenda. I was so accustomed to his continual generosity that I had never really thought about what he wanted to talk about. He was a king, but it seemed like he had made our times all about me. I experienced a new emotion that day: conviction without condemnation. His words gently pricked at my heart, revealing my foolishness yet not compelling me to hide. I never experienced this feeling on the streets. I always tried to stay out of trouble, and I only stole if I was unusually desperate for food. Typically, I only apologized if I was caught or if someone was screaming at me.

The king "caught" me in my selfishness, yet I actually welcomed this emotion of conviction to which I was unaccustomed. I had become somewhat spoiled and self-focused in my newfound role as the king's son. I had stopped thinking about what he wanted to teach me, and I started expecting him to take me where I wanted to go. I wasn't sure *what* he wanted, but I knew I didn't want to spend the rest of my life just trying to get my way. I would grow to understand that the king always made our times about me, yet they weren't just about me.

I didn't lose fascination with the War Room after that day, but I found out that there was more to learn about the palace—and the kingdom for that matter—than just warfare. Having never experienced anything purposeful or awe inspiring, I was inclined to cling to my first encounter with true meaning and make that the pinnacle experience to which all others would have to live up to. I wrongly assumed the other places in the palace and kingdom would bore me and pale in comparison to the War Room. Maybe I feared that if we left that room the king himself would one day become boring to me, and that scared me more than anything else.

After pondering all of this, I turned my attention to the king expecting to see him disappointed with my immaturity. However, instead of being disappointed, he was greatly anticipating what he had in store for me next. He opened the doorway at the end of the War Room and stepped into a magnificent throne room. It was larger than most houses and was covered wall to wall with a luxurious, plush, red carpet. Across the center of the back of the room were several steps leading up to a majestic golden throne. The room was beautiful and far more spacious than how I had envisioned a throne room.

I always expected a throne room to have a crowd of advisers, officials, and court servants lining the way to the king as seen in the movies. But this room was peaceful and empty except for the throne, the red carpet, and, of course, the king and me.[3]

The king approached the throne, sat on it, picked me up, and put me on his lap. I had never sat on someone's lap, but it seemed like a natural thing for a father to place his son on his lap. While I was resting in his arms, the king looked at me with deep love in his eyes. Not knowing love previously, I didn't know how to respond or react. I began to sense that he wanted me to look into his eyes. I knew he loved me, but it was unnatural for me to look into his eyes. Up to this point in my life, the only time I was ever required to make direct eye contact was after getting caught stealing on the streets. Some of the store owners who witnessed me stealing would grab my face in order to prevent me from looking away and demand I look them in the eyes as they yelled at me. So direct eye contact had never had a positive connotation for me.

Nevertheless, I mustered the courage to return the king's gaze. Maybe it seems strange to use the term "courage" in the context of looking at someone who loves you, but that simple act required exactly that. As I looked at him, I witnessed his love for me. I had not known him long, yet his love for me was so palpable and penetrating. I still wasn't sure how he could love me so much when I felt like he was still just getting to know me. But, either way, I took in as much of his love as I could that day. And, beyond feeling loved, for the first time in my life, I felt safe. No street bully, angry shop owner, or any instigator from my old street life could ever steal this newfound security and serenity. For the rest of my life, I would be protected by the most powerful and loving person in the kingdom. This was pure bliss.

After a long time of silent peace, the king led me down the steps onto the red carpet. He took my hand and began to dance across the throne room, leading me each step along the way. Despite never taking a dance lesson in my life, I danced freely with him, perfectly in step with his every move. Miraculously, I instantly possessed his polished dancing skills, and neither of us had to be meticulously focused on the dance steps. Instead, carefree and brimming with joy, we enthusiastically spun and twirled throughout the room. Previously neutral to the idea of dancing due to never having the experience, it now seemed like the most fun thing I could ever do. In fact, it was pure joy.[4]

Orphans do not have any reference for the peace, joy, freedom, and safety that I experienced with such intensity. As an orphan, I had only known the "adventure" of survival. As a result of this one dance, I transitioned from being an orphan just trying to live through the day to being a son tasting of what it really means to be alive. It's funny to think that just a few days prior the pinnacle of happiness involved hearing old war stories. A thousand of the greatest war stories paled in comparison to this moment with the king.

Hall of Fame

One day, the king invited me to take a walk with him. He led me to a door in the front left side of the throne room. Behind the door, which I somehow previously failed to notice, lay a magnificent hallway with tall, thick pillars on each side extending to a high, arching ceiling. At the top of the walls, just below the start of the arch of the ceiling, rested exquisitely framed portraits. These fascinating portraits of individual men and women lined the top of each wall along the entire length of the hallway.

While I didn't know the stories behind these paintings, each image emanated the greatness of the individual. Each man and woman exuded a depth of character and historical significance. It was as if the paintings could speak, filling the corridor with living testimonies.

Although I was not able to discern the specifics of their victories, each one had performed great exploits in the kingdom.

I loved walking through this hallway. Simply seeing the faces of these great ones filled me with wonder. I longed to leave a legacy as these had but assumed this would be highly unlikely. No one ever expected much from my life, and, until now, I had aligned myself with those low expectations. There was a comfort in knowing that regardless of whether or not I did anything great in life at least I was a son of the king. Yet, after months of meandering through the hall, I now possessed a glimmer of hope that I could one day be like the men and women in those paintings.

The king knew that I loved to gaze at the faces of the kingdom's greatest heroes. He never rebuked me for desiring to be great. As we walked the hall one day, I could not hold back my curiosity any longer and asked him, "What did they do? How did they get to have their portraits hung in the Hall of Fame? What made *them* so great?"

The king smiled at me, knowing I wanted to be like them, and answered, "These ones were great because they walked with me every day."

I was waiting for him to augment his comment with some specifications or additional credentials, but that is all the criteria he offered. He continued walking.

"Really?" I wondered to myself, "That doesn't seem that great! Isn't that what I do every day?"

It certainly didn't seem like what I was doing was anything laudable or exemplary. Who would resist the opportunity to spend every day with the king of the whole land?

"I don't understand," I said, not protesting but looking for some further clarification.

"These ones walked with me every day," he continued. "Many others have begun their journey by walking right here with me in this palace. They initially plan on doing this for life but soon lose sight of me. Some only walked with me as long as I stayed in the palace. Others found other interests outside of the palace and forgot me even though I was their father. These ones," he pointed back to those on the wall, "walked with me wherever I went. They shared everything with me, and I shared everything with them." Then, turning to me, he affirmed, "That is all you have to do to be the greatest in the kingdom."[5]

I was astonished. It seemed so simple, too simple almost. Yet, seeing the grandeur of these men and women, I knew the greatness of their journeys with the king. Furthermore, I was amazed at the king's declaration that I could be among the greatest in the kingdom. While I tried not to dwell on it too much, the thought of having my portrait in the Hall of Fame played in my mind for years. Even though the pathway to greatness—despite the king's explanation—was still somewhat nebulous in my mind, I determined I could never settle for anything else.

Yes, what the king told me that day was the truth. The desire grew in me each day to walk with the king wherever he went. I had no idea what to expect outside the palace, but, if he chose to be outside the palace, I yearned to be with him in that place. I knew the king couldn't just hang around the palace all year. After all, he was a king. Battles would arise, challenges would surface, and surprises would surely await us. Certainly, if I was going to follow his footsteps, I needed some training. I had no idea what I was getting myself into, but, for better or worse, I was determined to follow the king no matter where he went.

Ghost-boys

One day, I entered the throne room again to sit on the king's lap. After my first day in the throne room, this became a welcomed routine for us. Despite all the king's responsibilities to his kingdom, he never failed to make time to let me sit with him. The joy, comfort, tranquility, and safety I felt the first moment in his lap never diminished over time.

On this particular day, as he held me, I began to become aware of boys in the courtyard looking in on us. I became slightly embarrassed since, even though I was still young, it didn't seem like the cool thing to be sitting on my dad's lap. To make matters worse, it appeared from the corner of my eye that they were sneering at me. The more self-conscious I grew, the more the boys advanced toward us. I don't know if the throne room became smaller, or the courtyard crept closer to the throne. Either way, I was progressively more distracted by these boys.[6]

Eventually, although I knew the king wanted me to look in his eyes, I became too aware of those viewing the scene. Embarrassed, I turned from the king to observe these onlookers. I figured I could quickly "size them up" to see if I should worry about their opinions of me. They appeared to be boys around my age. Despite neither having met them nor knowing where they came from, I desired their approval. Under their watchful eyes, I felt childish and ashamed while sitting on the king's lap. Their whispering among themselves as they stared at me was not helping my self-esteem either.

I quickly realized that these were not typical boys. Rather than running toward us, the boys floated swiftly through the courtyard to the edge of the throne room as if they were ghosts rather than boys. Each "ghost-boy" would whisk through the air, point his finger, and then mock me for sitting on the king's lap. As soon as I noticed one, he would speed away back to the courtyard.

While I was concerned about my reputation, the king was determined to not allow anything detract from my time with him. He was totally unconcerned with the boys laughing at us but knew that their words and actions were impacting me. I soon saw why they were fleeing as quickly as they came. As one would draw near, the king would take his eyes off of me momentarily and give the ghost-boy a stern glance. As soon as the king looked at one, the boy would cackle like a hyena and then flee in fear for the courtyard. Boy after boy would approach to mock me only to see the king's face and flee as if fleeing for his life.

It's quite a joyful sight to see your dad step in and terrify those who harass you. On the streets, I had no dad to protect me, so this was especially gratifying for me. I felt like yelling out, "Yeah! That's what I thought!" I wanted to harass them in return as they fled. Maybe I was a tad overconfident, but I was excited about finally having someone stick up for me and having others run *from me* in fear. Yet, even though the king and I were the "winners" that day, I was still disturbed by these boys. I knew the king loved me, but I still wanted the other kids my age to like me.

"What am I supposed to do, King?" I asked him. "It's really hard to concentrate on you and enjoy my time with you when I keep getting made fun of by others my age."

"My son," he said with sincerity, "these ones will always be here. They are not just near the throne room; they are throughout the entire kingdom.[7] Just as I will be with you wherever you go, so they too will be with you wherever you go. But they are cowards, and they have no hold on you. Haven't you seen how terrified they are when they see my eyes? As scared as you are of them, they are far more scared of not just me but you because you are with me."

I had to train myself to not be distracted by them, and, eventually, my fear of these ghost-boys waned and disappeared. I simply had to keep looking to the king and looking where he was looking. I can only assume these boys continued their routine day after day because I stopped noticing them. I simply enjoyed the love of the king too much and didn't have time to spend my life worrying about ghost-boys.

I could have sat on the king's lap looking into his eyes forever. I knew that no matter what lay ahead nothing would be better than being with the king. Additionally, I assumed I had already learned the greatest lessons in the kingdom—not to demand my own way, not to fear others, and to enjoy every moment with the king. What else could I learn?

Little did I know, my journey was just beginning.

3

TRAINING GROUNDS

It was time to train. I exited through the side of the palace and entered a large field filled with weapon stations designed for training soldiers. I scanned the field, taking note of areas for sword fighting, tracks for jousting, targets for archery, and more. Many young warriors-in-training were consumed with their various practice combat exercises.

"I have brought you into my palace as a son," the king said, "but I also brought you in as a warrior for me." It seemed like handling a sword was a logical place to begin, so I headed over to the station with the rack of swords. I began, as all do, with the basics—how to hold the sword, swing it properly, and wield it without hurting myself in the process. I was surprised to see that some of the most experienced warriors, even after years of training, still had not learned to avoid cutting themselves with their own swords. Some even inflicted more wounds on themselves or their fellow soldiers than the enemy ever would.

After several months of sword training, I now faced a more daunting challenge: jousting. As every warrior knows, although handling a weapon presents challenges, managing it while mounted on horseback is an altogether different endeavor. Furthermore, I feared getting slammed in the chest or knocked off the horse onto my back. As I began to imagine various potential scenarios, the intimidation began to set in. The king spoke plainly to me, "I'm telling you right now, you *will* get knocked off your horse."

Even though I knew this was not the typical way to encourage a timid novice, I knew I needed to hear this. I had become increasingly anxious by fixating on the fear of pain rather than the task at hand. Without even stopping to ponder what I needed to do to succeed, I had already dwelt on the potential to fail.

"Many joust simply to not get knocked off their horse," the king added. "Do not aim not to lose. Joust to win."

I greatly valued these times of training with the king. Of course, the previous lessons I had gleaned in the War Room laid a critical foundation for my life. I had gained vital insight into battle tactics as well as instructions in steering clear of the mistakes of past warriors. Many of their miscues seemed so obviously foolish to me in hindsight. However, the king taught me that many of these great ones fell into the snares of *their generation*. Each generation had its own set of ensnarements that seduced some of the king's greatest fighters. If I simply memorized the details of past failures but did not increase in wisdom from them, I would be susceptible to the pitfalls of *my generation*. While many of the king's and the enemy's tactics remained the same throughout the history of the kingdom, the enemy customized traps for each new breed of the king's warriors. These traps looked different on the outside, which is one reason why so many fell, but the basic strategies never really changed. To the great consternation of the king, many of his sons prided themselves in avoiding yesterday's downfalls, while simultaneously walking headlong into the demises of today. This arrogance was often coupled with an exaltation of whoever these sons deemed heroes of the past.[8]

As I practiced day in and day out with the king, I slowly became aware of just how many other warriors were training around us. It's quite difficult to describe how one can slowly recognize someone else's presence, especially when hundreds of others are in close proximity. However, this gradual realization occurred regularly. Every new season in my life seemed like it was just the king and I experiencing it.

Then I would realize a few others around me and eventually be cognizant of a whole gathering of his sons that had been participating all along. Most of us were by nature largely unaware of those around us. I suppose that because the king trained me with such personalized devotion I imagined we had the whole grounds to ourselves. Nonetheless, many of the palace warriors labored daily in preparation for the battles ahead.

Eventually, the continual training lost its luster. Since we were only practicing and not fighting a real enemy, these endless repetitions with no consequences for failure began to bore me. One day, after several hours of laborious training, I began to wonder, "Do I really have to train one hundred percent? This is tiring, and it's the same thing over and over. I have been training for months. I'll know what to do in battle. Besides, I'm getting worn out. Of course I'll give it my all on the day of the battle, but I might as well conserve my energy and take it easy."

"Every day is to be taken very seriously," the king interjected, intercepting my thoughts. "If you do not work diligently each day in the preparation stage, don't even bother going out to fight on the day of battle." He also explained that in a mysterious way this training *was* part of the great battle against the enemy. I didn't fully understand but had learned enough by now to know the king knew what he was talking about. He was not, after all, just a benevolent monarch. He was also a mastermind of war.

As the training progressed, I moved on to other areas such as archery and canoeing. I particularly enjoyed rowing, although it seemed more like a hobby than an element of war. The warriors spent a lot of time practicing escaping, which seemed rather cowardly to me. However, the king told me that for even the greatest warriors there is a time to escape. "This is not a matter of cowardice. You must discern which battles you can win and only fight those to which I have called you. I have never called any of my sons to fight a battle they will not win.[9] Furthermore," he added, "it doesn't matter how great of a swordsman you are if you cannot outrow your enemy when it's time to flee."

I came to understand that there was a manual for all of this, which was full of proper fighting techniques, steps for taking a soldier from one stage of training to another, and instructions on when it was time to leave the training grounds and go out into battle. After being sent out, the wisest and most successful warriors would always return to be further equipped. The king's top adviser, Suelo, would take all the sons through the training manual again and again. Even the greatest warriors continued to gain new techniques from these sessions. Suelo possessed the same knowledge as the king, and the manual contained everything that a son needed to know about fighting. Thus, Suelo taking us through the fighting manual was exactly the same as being taught by the king.[10] Numerous other soldiers were training at the same time, and I began to feel like I was losing the personal dimension of my time with the king. The king explained to me the importance of growing with the other sons and learning while strengthening each other. I was not to avoid others just so I could spend more time alone with the king. The truth of the matter was that any time I was with them I was with the king.

I watched how the greatest and most mature warriors focused not just on their own training but also on the progress of other warriors. They would take note of others' weaknesses so they could then build them up to their same level of greatness. I was grateful for these old warriors because, even though they gained a great reputation for the battles they won, they were concerned about the young ones winning great battles in the future. They easily could have started an "Old Warriors Club" and sat around all day talking about all the great battles they had won, and no one would have faulted them for it. Yet, their focus on the younger and untrained ones made sense for, as everyone knows, no one goes into battle alone. The greatest swordsman in the world would not last long fighting alongside an army of amateur soldiers.

The greatest fighters would see not only the weaknesses of the young trainees but also their potential. Many of these sons would become greater than the wise warriors who trained them. Had the great warriors known capable older warriors like themselves in their younger years, they would have become even greater. It took humility, but the greatest assets to the kingdom were not those who could excel in *one* area[11] but those who could help others to excel in *many* areas.

Although I dedicated myself to the training the king established for me, I also took note of the habits of fellow warriors. After the initial training period, many began to spend all their time honing one particular skill. They excelled beyond others in this one area yet lagged far behind even beginners in other areas. Specialization was needed to some extent, but the motivation for their preoccupation with a single skill was simple: pride.

Other warriors, especially younger ones, continued to be impressed by any warrior who had great skill in one area. I watched one experienced warrior masterfully wield his sword, thereby amazing a group of impressionable new warriors. He moved his sword with a level of expertise beyond anything I had attained in my training. Amazed at his talent, the onlookers began joking with one another about a million years of practice not being sufficient enough to attain to his skill level. I quickly discerned that this veteran warrior was not training them; he was entertaining them. His display of techniques appeared impressive from the outside but failed to be productive in the long run. The king affirmed my concerns, "His tricks are not practical for actually fighting a battle. His 'skills' not only jeopardize himself but also the other warriors around him. He does not even remember how to properly use a shield and often goes into battle with no armor. His sword will do him little good when the fiery arrows of the enemy head his way. Worse yet, he is training the younger ones to follow in his footsteps."

I purposed in my heart that day, "No matter what happens, I must become a complete warrior!" I turned to my trainer. "Please, King," I pleaded with him, "don't ever let me become one dimensional!" I didn't hear a reply from him but had no doubt as to his heart on the matter. This was the kind of warrior's request he loved to fulfill.

I also noticed sects and separated groups of sons in the training grounds. Many of these factions rallied around one or two sons that had trained longer than they had. They gave up meeting with the entire army as well as the training sessions with Suelo. When I asked the king about this, he answered, "The leaders of the factions are mostly teaching accurately from what they learned from Suelo in their early days of training. They were so impacted by these teachings that they have made these few principles the only concepts that matter. But they are no longer able to accept most of what I teach the other sons because it does not fit their paradigm. Their foundations are great, but who wants to live in a house with just a foundation? They believe they are doing me a favor by teaching the younger ones this 'secret knowledge,' but I would have taught it to them anyway and taught it better. And I would not have left them with only the basics."

These teachers who were determined to have their own following caused much division in the camp. I asked the king why he kept these ones and still allowed them to remain on the palace grounds since it seemed very counterproductive to our training. He simply said, "I love my sons." I felt a little foolish that I was so quick to exile my brothers. My love was not yet like the king's. He continued, "And, besides, most of what they are teaching *is* what I taught them. It's just that they make those few teachings out to be the whole way of fighting. I have been very patient with them."

I knew the king had been patient with me. I began to reminisce when I first entered the palace. I often tried to get my way, and I only wanted to see what I wanted to see rather than what the king wanted to show me. I had behaved like these teachers: I wanted to visit the same places every day. Fortunately, the king patiently showed me that he had so much more for me. Life with the king involves one great revelation after another.[12] I compare it to a young child who is the son of a world-class chef. As he moves from baby food to adult food, his father daily introduces the child to one savory new taste after another.

Thinking about how good it was to be trained by the king, I became curious as to how the enemy trained his sons. (The enemy's camp was located beyond the mountains that separated the two kingdoms.) The king explained, "The enemy trains through threats, secret pacts, fear of punishment, and many promises of rewards, which spark jealousy among his recruits. These tactics work very well for him. Jealousy is as unyielding as the grave. It is a powerful motivator for his sons."

These did not seem like effective methods for training an army, but I realized that hatred was a very powerful tool, especially in warfare. After all, what commander focuses his battle preparation talks on how to love the opposing army more? The king also said that if one judged by mere appearance, the king's own techniques and the enemy's (foreign kings) techniques often looked very similar and that many could not even discern the difference. But the motivation behind the techniques was far different, and the end result of applying these tactics over the course of a lifetime was light years apart.

I remembered that when I first arrived at the palace the king had told me that what was most important was to know him and love him. I still was unsure how I would find time to get to know the king more if I was training and fighting all day. He responded to my internal uncertainty stating that the palace held three feasts a day and that these gatherings were special times for all the sons to collectively spend with the king. Additionally, he said that, unlike in other kingdoms where it was impossible to spend a whole day in personal time with a friend while simultaneously undergoing intense training, it was possible in this kingdom to spend very personal time with the king in the midst of intense labor. "Everything is possible in my kingdom," he said proudly.

I once again considered the great ones who had gone before us. Many of those currently in our camp yearned for what those great ones possessed, and they desired to attain what those great ones had achieved, but they did little about it. In fact, many wanted to replicate the exact same feats in the same way that previous warriors had accomplished them. But a true warrior will find the battles that need to be won in his own day and then lead others in victory. The king told me that all he required of me was to fully dedicate myself to the training each day and take every lesson seriously. He concluded by saying, "The training is an equally important part of the battle as the actual battle itself."

4

THE GARDEN

The king approached me and asked, "Won't you take a walk with me in the garden?" I asked, not expecting an answer, "There's a garden in this palace?" As we walked, I saw chest-high bushes on the left, knee-high bushes on the right, and a tall tree straight ahead. All had fruit on them. I asked why some were more noticeable like the tall tree. I don't think I received an answer. I, along with the other sons, sometimes learned more effectively when he gave us no reply at all and rather allowed us to simply observe. I began to see that some fruit was hidden and some was visible. I asked why this was the case but soon saw that it was not critical that fruit be readily noticeable. What was important, the king told me, was that the fruit was ripe and pleasing to the gardener. I thought about how the fruit needed proper nurturing and care. I noticed that the fruit on the tall, conspicuous trees had required more time to develop. The process of absorbing water and minerals and transferring them from the roots to the fruit was time consuming. Though glorious in stature now, this tree began like any other plant with a few roots in the dirt.

The fruit bushes were in need of upkeep, and the king informed me that he was to teach me how to prune, garden, and nurture these bushes. I knew his gardening abilities far surpassed mine. As a result, I didn't understand why he wanted to include me in the process, especially since the young fruit was so fragile. Apparently, the king not only considered it worth the risk to involve me in his work, but he genuinely wanted me to partner with him in tending the garden. Also, I understood that the king did not want me to be a spoiled son who had everything given to him without having to work for it. Without any prior horticultural experience, I would have to join him each day to learn how to properly garden.

To nurture the bushes—he assigned me to the chest-high bushes on the left—I needed to obtain the necessary daily food, water, and tools. Since only the king had access to where the materials were stored, I would have to depend on the king for the tools I needed each day. As time went on, I did not need the king constantly by my side to garden, and he had other responsibilities.

After a while, I wanted to do more than just garden. I asked the king, "Can't I go with you, and we can garden together?" He was my greatest joy, and, although gardening and seeing the fruit of my labor was fulfilling, I wanted to be with him. Upon looking at him, I could see that this was what he wanted me to desire. By having me labor on my own, he was testing my heart. Did I want to do work for him, or did I want to work *with* him?[13]

As we co-labored for many days, I began to wonder, "Doesn't a master teach an apprentice all he knows?" I reasoned to myself, "Won't I eventually know as much as he does if I keep working with him?" This seemed logical since it happens all the time with people of many different trades, but it didn't seem possible that I would ever know as much as the king. He answered my internal monologue by telling me that he knew everything about the fruit—its origin, its history, and even its composition. Thus, his knowledge would always be more comprehensive than mine, but he would impart to me his understanding of cultivating fruits. His intent was that I would grow to be an expert gardener and tend the garden just like he had. Also, a mystery of his garden was that even if someone planted a bush and another watered it every day, it was always the king who made it grow.

One day, as I entered the garden, the king told me that he would give me my own fruit bush and that I would no longer just tend what he and others had planted. Because I had been responsible in tending to my assigned bushes, he would give me my very own bush. When he told me this, I was so filled with honor and joy. I felt like a little child receiving his first pet.[14] I couldn't believe the king would trust me to place seeds and nurture them into a mature bush. All I could think to do was bow before him in reverence for being given such a great responsibility. Any gift the king gives causes intense gratitude and carries far greater worth inside the palace than it does in the surrounding kingdom.

I learned many things from having my own bush that I had not gleaned when I just tended others' gardens. I learned to independently evaluate the bush and its fruit and respond by providing the appropriate nutrients, water, or sunlight. Later, I learned about repellents to keep away flies and predators, which would destroy the fruit. However, the king taught me that I was not to only focus on keeping flies away. Some sons would spend too much time keeping flies away. As a result, they forgot to ever properly nurture the fruit. The fruit was protected from the outside while it withered from within.

I often wondered why the king even allowed flies in his kingdom in the first place and permitted them to land on his fruit. The fruit became damaged from the flies. I knew he could destroy them, so why didn't he? As usual, I knew he saw something that I didn't. I also wondered what happened to the fruit ripe for picking. I assumed it was used to nourish the sons of the king and that its seeds were taken elsewhere to grow more fruit.

I also saw other unripened fruit, but it was detached from the vine. Although it looked good at first, no one picked it up to eat it. It quickly withered and died without nourishment. The king was the only one who could take this dying fruit and reattach it to the vine.

I wondered why I never saw anyone else in the garden though the work of many others was apparent. The king then opened my eyes to see thousands of workers gardening the bushes that he had given them. It was amazing how the king gave undivided attention to each worker and spent hours training each one. Yet, having done this thousands of times before, his training was so intimate[15] and catered to the specific concepts that each individual personally needed to learn. He also opened my eyes to see that many of the bushes had their growth stunted by weeds entwined in their branches. As with the flies, the king allowed this to take place. In my mind, this didn't seem like a shrewd practice, but he let me know that at harvest time he would pick all the fruit and then pluck out the weeds and throw them away. At the harvest, some of the fruit was clearly less ripe because of the weeds' interference. As I questioned this in my head, I saw the king turn and smile at me as if to gently indicate, "I know what you're thinking. Just trust me."

At harvest time, I saw that some of the fruit had far more seeds inside of them than others. I wondered if I should cease tending this latter fruit since it had minimal reproducing capabilities. However, much of the fruit that had the fewest seeds tasted the sweetest. Also, much of the smallest fruit was most satisfying to the sons of the king. I came to understand that I would be tending fruit my whole life and that it would be a good idea to grow many different types and sizes of fruit. I also saw that I wasn't required to plant all of the seeds, but, instead, the wind would often carry them to other fertile grounds. From there, they would mature without anyone tending them.

My time in the palace garden was a special season for me. Some of my most cherished moments with the king took place here. Because I learned so many invaluable lessons in the garden, I asked the king, "What are the most important lessons to remember from my time here?"

He highlighted three points: "First, you must come to get tools, food, and water from me every day. You will never be able to get these on your own. Next, you must not get so caught up in gardening that you forget why I brought you to the palace in the first place. You were an orphan, and I brought you into the palace to be with me and to be my son. Finally, any success you have in this garden comes from my tools and my knowledge, and, even with all of your proper gardening techniques, I alone make the garden grow."

5

THE FEAST

The king called a great feast. Men from all over the palace gathered to celebrate. A huge banquet table arrayed with gourmet foods and exquisite place settings stood before us. The king sat at the head of the table while the sons filled in the rest of the seats. I sensed that not only a great feast would ensue but great fellowship as well. Since he was better than any banquet, I asked the king why we needed food in the first place. It seemed to me that being with the king in addition to being with the other sons was what everyone was most looking forward to. He said the food was there to remind us of our hunger for fellowship with each other. Since the day I entered the palace, I was continually aware of my hunger to be with the king but had never associated this hunger with being with the king's sons. Yet, now, at this table, we were drawn by an inexplicable hunger to spend time with each other.

As we ate, many conversations naturally arose between sons throughout the banquet hall. Despite the myriad of conversations at the table, it was as if each was the only one taking place in the room. People maintained eye contact and were entirely undistracted by the surrounding dialogue. This happened all across the banquet hall in groups of twos, threes, and fours. Meanwhile, the most popular guest at the table, the king, simply sat and proudly treasured his sons enjoying each other.

Unaware until now, I gradually realized that I was surrounded by nobles at the table. Each noble son was adorned in finely woven apparel of earthy colors—reds, greens, oranges, and the like. Also, each carried an air of greatness while banqueting in the presence of the king. I'm sure their accomplishments and accolades were endless, yet no one was interested in bragging about their own feats. Instead, they were eager get to know their fellow brothers more. Besides, not one at the table was of noble birth, and each knew that they did not deserve to be there.

As we continued to enjoy the feast, there arose a strange and increasing awareness of the need for someone to lay down his life. A man to my right was the first to volunteer, declaring to the entire room, "I will lay down my life for you." The man clearly did not offer his life out of obligation. Then, a man to my left also declared, "I will lay down my life for you." And soon, one by one, this one phrase echoed from each mouth across the banquet hall. Although we felt a tight-knit camaraderie before this moment, the additional element of sacrifice brought us to a whole new level of unity.

I had always longed for the intimacy in friendship I now experienced. Because I'm an idealist, I hadn't previously acknowledged my need for this kind of friendship. I had always told myself that all I need is the king. Yet, in my zeal to be the palace's best son, whatever that means, I spent all of my time thinking about the king and considered hanging out with the other sons to be of lesser value. Maybe I thought that spending time having fun with others was for the less committed. But, as I sat here enjoying my brothers, I knew the king was showing us a whole new way to relate to him: by relating to each other. It was as if talking with them was talking to the king. And the king was not the only one who would willingly sacrifice for me. I was surrounded by brothers who would lay down their lives for me. It was one of the most secure feelings anyone could ever know.

As I sat there satisfied by the food and the friendship, I thought about how this fulfillment was too good to not share with others. I began to feel selfish since I knew there were so many outside the palace living empty lives, ignorant of the realities of what they could experience as a son of the king. How could I sit here feasting with my friends without a care in the world while so many were living the miserable life I once knew all too well? It didn't seem right.

"Don't even bother going out there if you're not friends with those in here," the king told me.

"Really?" I thought to myself. I assumed he was trying to make a point, but it seemed overstated. The king, knowing my thoughts, didn't seem to be offended by my question.

He continued to explain to me that loving my brothers is loving him. If I didn't love my brothers at the banquet table, I didn't really love the king. Some sons might like the concept of being around the king, but, if they really loved him, it was impossible for them to resist loving his other sons.

"Don't even try it!" he said conclusively to the whole table, referencing the futility of attempting to love the king without loving his sons, to which the group let out a laugh.

Knowing I was still curious about the implications of this principle, he then showed me what happened to those who focused solely on recruiting others to the palace while neglecting the daily banquets. To them, meeting with their brothers was a mere rote requirement. In their minds, communal feasting didn't seem to have much value nor did it have any influence on their effectiveness outside the palace. I did see a number of them initially attend the feasts, but I believe this was merely a temporary courtesy to the king. They spent much of their time discussing strategies on how they could next "position" the king in a conversation with someone outside the palace. I believe they lived their whole lives constantly formulating new recruitment tactics in the backs of their minds.

As I watched these sons, I was surprised that they not only stopped meeting with their brothers at the table, they even stopped meeting with the king himself. This was very surprising to me. For all the hours that they talked *about* the king, it only seemed natural to at least occasionally talk *with* the king! They began taking trips outside the palace and not coming back in at night. At first they would sleep in the courtyard, then outside the gates, and, eventually, they would go days without returning to the palace. Still, every day, they would carry on long conversations about the king with those outside the palace or with other sons who had not visited in a while.

It was truly amazing how much they knew about the king for having spent so little time with him. I would occasionally listen to them and think, "How do they know that? I didn't even know that about the king, and I've been hanging out with him for years!" And it seemed the entire palace knew that they were correct in many of the things that they said.

Unfortunately, despite all of the knowledge these brothers of mine possessed, their words were empty and void of life. It was quite grieving to witness. The love of the king, the joy of the palace, and the efficacy of the training did not motivate these sons to draw others to the palace. Instead, they were continually driven by the single thought, "I'm right!" This one assertion fueled everything they did and provided them the strength to spend weeks away from the palace. Some were even quite successful in convincing others to at least believe that the king was real. (Surprisingly, some in the kingdom still refused to believe that the king existed.) Their followers were no different, though. They became experts in convincing others that their teachers' beliefs about the king were correct. Eventually, however, these followers abandoned loyalty to their teachers' philosophies and steered listeners toward the supremacy of their own beliefs.

This group of "city dwellers," as I came to call them, had an odd sense of unity among themselves. Despite their propensity to satisfy their own egos, something internally drove them to rally around certain beliefs and teachings. I'm not sure how much they actually liked each other, but they always seemed to huddle close together when topics arose of which they were particularly fond. After several generations, some would even spend their whole lives without even visiting the palace. More surprisingly, many even began teaching that it was not possible to go to the palace or meet the king! I couldn't believe it!

Sitting in the palace, I was incredulous hearing these men tell others that it was impossible to go to the palace!

"Are they really even sons?" I asked the king. "How could they possibly believe this stuff about you? How can they be your son if they've never been to the palace and met you?"

"They are my sons," he affirmed. "I do occasionally go visit them, so they have met me. I even speak to them and talk with them, which is why their teachings are prevented from being too far off. But they view me as just that—a teaching. So, despite being watered down and filtered through their limited channels of reasoning, it is I who have taught them."

As the king explained his relationship with these sons, it was evident that he clearly loved them. I was less compassionate and wondered why the king even bothered to invest in these distant sons. I clearly saw his heart that day: He loved with all his heart even the sons farthest from the palace who least reflected who he truly is.

Having seen enough of those that went out without returning to the daily banquets, I was eager to see what happened to those who loved to feast. "If those that don't even come to the palace have had success," I wondered to myself, "what will happen when those feasting daily with the king and his sons seek out others to bring in to the palace?" The king, never the one to disappoint, read my thoughts and whispered, "Come on. Let me show you."

6

FILLED UP, SENT OUT

After feasting for days with his children, the king sent them throughout the kingdom to invite others to come to the palace. I was eager to see how their methods differed from the city dwellers who neglected the daily feasts at the banqueting table. Before the sons departed, the king gave them specific directions: "Do not focus on or cater your message to those on the left or the right, but speak to those in the middle."[16] I questioned this strategy as I watched the scene unfold because it seemed to conflict with the king's own expressed heart for all in his kingdom to come to the palace. I was certain he had some reason for his instructions, but, whatever they were, they seemed contradictory to his character.

I saw a "sent one" travel far away from the palace and enter a neighborhood. Many people gathered outside a market place and engaged in lively conversation. The crowd of people was divided into three groups. On the left were ones who, from a distance, looked like rabid dogs but on closer inspection turned out to be people. On the right were community religious leaders, dressed in long, flowing white robes with various ornate decorations. In between these two opposing groups stood the majority of people, the commoners.

One son listened to the king and ventured toward the common people in the middle of the crowd. As he spoke of the king, the crowd was perplexed. It wasn't that they disagreed; it was just that the life of the palace was so foreign to them. Their everyday lives contrasted greatly with the reality of the palace being presented to them. As the son addressed those in the middle of the crowd, many on the left and right also congregated to listen. In fact, everywhere he spoke, he did not have to pursue those on the left or the right. He simply spoke to the common people, and the rabid dogs and the religious leaders always eventually gathered.

The king also showed me what would happen if the son did not heed his advice as to where to keep his focus. The ones on the left were experts at getting a reaction out of the son. They continually assaulted him with words, mocked his message, and even took personal shots at his character. He was blindsided by the allegations and was quickly drawn into counterattacks. Fear quickly crept into the son's heart—after all, these mockers had the appearance of rabid dogs, especially when they were at the height of their attacks. Because the son now spent so much time answering his critics, the critics, instead of the king, were the ones setting the agenda for the discussions each day. Eventually, after continuous arguing, he dedicated the majority of his time defending his own character, attempting to convince them that his motives were not impure. Because the mockers dictated the content of the dialogue, the message of the king was quickly forfeited.

Those on the right had different means for distracting the son's focus but achieved similar results as those on the left. The men in the flowing white robes spent many hours teaching the people all sorts of laws and moral codes. It seemed they continually found new teachings based on their own interpretation and ever morphing applications of the kingdom's laws. As a result, the common people grew totally dependent on the leaders and ceased to seek truth for themselves. This was exactly what the leaders were hoping for.

The religious leaders also placed great emphasis on the buildings where people gathered for religious ceremonies. Again, the people bought into this system and felt guilty if they did not frequent the building.[17] I'm not sure they knew why they were supposed to go to the building, but the leaders were seasoned experts at subtly guilt-tripping people into attending. The people even began putting guilt trips on each other for not attending even though they didn't know why they went. Some managed to not feel guilty if they sent their children even if they did not visit the building themselves.

As the son attempted to reach out to the religious leaders, they initially ignored him. However, when he even briefly captured the audience's attention, the leaders became jealous. They immediately engaged the son and began rigorously and systematically confronting with him. Surprisingly, the moral codes and standards of the son and the leaders did not differ significantly. There were minor variations, but the people often had trouble distinguishing what separated the son's standards from the leaders'. The constant debating took its toll on the son, and he soon grew too weary to continue his mission. The worst part of this scenario was that the life and the passion of the son were sapped from him. Because of the overemphasis on moral codes and regulations, his joy of being with the king and sharing the realities of the kingdom quickly dissipated. Once again, as when the son focused on reaching those on the left, he allowed others to establish the agenda.

I then watched a different scenario in which this son obeyed the king and directed his attention toward the common people in the middle. He spoke of the reality of the palace and the joy of continually feasting with the king. Day after day, he proclaimed that the life of the palace far surpassed anything the rest of the kingdom offered. At the end of each talk, the people marveled at how the man spoke with such confidence and authority. Previously, many of the townspeople believed in the palace's existence, but their former notion was more abstract and theoretical than a practical reality. The palace had seemed too good to be true, but the son's wise and refreshing message stirred many hearts to view the king as more than just a theory. Many hearts were awakened from their dormant state after years of numbness and lethargy.

I was intrigued by the differing responses that I perceived among the crowd as the son spoke. To some, everything he shared seemed like revolutionary concepts and utopian scenarios. Others were tempted to think the son was relying on hype. To me, the message was my daily experience—feasting with the king, training for battle, and dancing for hours in the throne room. Although he had the temptation to do so, when speaking of the king, the son had no need for hype. The reality of the infinite pleasures of the palace spoke for itself.

As I previously noticed, as the son focused on the people in the middle, those on the left and right quickly swarmed to the gathering. Ironically, even though those on the right or left didn't care at all about the common people, they continually labored to "protect the people" from the sons. The rabid dog-like people on the left relentlessly vilified the son and manipulated the emotions of the crowd. Those on the right were slower to speak and would often spend long hours at night discussing the inaccuracies of the son's message. Eventually, they rendered a verdict and announced to the people the "official decree" regarding the required response to the son's message. While those on the left were motivated by disdain, those on the right were fueled by jealousy.

Scores of townspeople were impacted by the son when he obeyed the king's instructions and stayed focused on the common people. Although many were influenced by the son's teaching, the king only showed me two specific examples of citizens accepting invitations to the palace. One of these men had been one of the religious leaders to the right in the crowd. As he listened in amazement day after day to the message, his heart was slowly awakened. Throughout his entire life, he had hoped that, someday, someone would journey to the palace, but he had never met anyone who had accomplished this feat. Reaching the palace was merely a theoretical possibility to him which seemed too good to be true. Even though he was uncertain of the palace's accessibility, he had longed for years for a tangible experience with it. He began to ask the son many questions, not to trap him as the other leaders did, but, instead, to learn. I saw that it took a significant amount of humility for the leader to glean from the son's wisdom. The religious leaders deemed ludicrous even a small hint of taking the son seriously. Thus, this man would often remove his white robes in order to sneak unnoticed into the crowds to hear the son. Despite the fear of his colleagues, the religious man's hunger for an experience with the reality of the palace was too great for him to ignore.

Eventually, the son personally invited this leader to come to the palace. The leader, whose name was Nic, was immediately filled with wonder and amazement at the prospect of visiting the palace. Nic still found it difficult to believe the son, yet he couldn't resist the opportunity to experience what he had so thoroughly and eloquently taught about for decades.

Another religious leader had also accepted the invitation. Not as enthusiastic as Nic, still intrigued by the palace, he followed a few steps behind Nic and the son. He accepted the invitation partially out of a desire to experience the palace but also because he was impressed by the son's authority, an authority his peers did not possess. As he drew near to the palace walls, he appeared to be overcome by a strange conviction. The man began listing off multiple reasons why he should not be granted entrance into the palace. "I'm not worthy to go in," he flatly stated. He then objected, "I've done too much wrong in my life." He added, "I'm too old. Let the children go in. They have their whole lives in front of them."

The son was unsuccessful in convincing the man to enter, so he only escorted Nic into the palace. The son notified the king of the other man's reluctance to enter. Immediately, the king left the palace to personally invite the hesitant religious leader into the palace. I was surprised by the king's quick departure since he generally sent his sons to invite others to the palace. Yet, even with a personal invitation from the king and assurance that the king would accept him, the man persisted in rejecting the king's offer.

It is always painful seeing someone in the kingdom entrenched in their refusal to accept the king. Every time I saw the king invite someone—whether through the sons or himself personally—a stream of joy-filled memories of coming to the palace in those early days would flood my mind. Then, a barrage of questions also followed. "Why would you reject such an offer? Can't you see how much better life is here than your former life? Can't you just give it a try or a test run or something?" I needed to ask the king about this.

The king responded to my inquiries as he explained, "Even though he gave the excuse that he was not worthy, in reality, he was bitter that I had not called him earlier in his life. 'Why didn't you send one of your sons to me when I was younger?' That's what he asked me. He blamed me for the fact that he had been teaching things about me his entire life that he now knows are not accurate. He also believes that if he had received this invitation when he was young he would have gladly welcomed it and spent his whole life in the palace. But, as it stands now, because of the confidence with which he has declared his former teachings, he deems his reputation in the community too much to give up. Too much is at stake for him now to accept my offer."

Sadly, the man departed and returned to his former life. Even though he knew full well that he was welcome in the palace, he was bitter at the king for the timing of the invitation and at Nic for entering the palace. I cannot be certain of this, but I heard that he returned to his former life and dove right back into teaching what he had always taught. He knew some of his descriptions of the palace and king were inaccurate, but he prioritized the people's adulation over truth even after having his eyes opened to the palace. The man was skilled at hiding it, but he spent the rest of his life full of bitterness at the king.

Unlike the religious man who refused to accept the king's invitation to enter the palace, Nic was filled with awe at every phase of the journey to the palace. Even his initial view from a distance of merely the top of the palace captivated him. However, even after beholding the palace with his own eyes, its existence and accessibility still seemed too good to be true. Nic was brought to the palace and immediately led to the fellowship table. He enjoyed the food but still was unable to fully engage in fellowship because he was soaking up the wonder of the entire experience. Day after day, he would come to the fellowship table and think to himself, "I just can't believe this is all true!"

I also saw that when the feasts were over, Nic would approach the king to ask him many questions. They would go on long walks through the hallway, often into the night, as he presented question after question to the king. His method of thinking was still partially patterned after his former life, but his curiosity and hunger for the things of the palace superseded any entrenched mindsets of the past.

One day, I saw Nic sitting at the banquet table as was his usual custom. He still felt like a child visiting a candy store for the first time. It seemed like those around him still appreciated the feasts, but their childlike awe had apparently faded to some degree as time progressed. Though I could not see the king at this time, it seemed he desired all of his sons to have the mindset of this former religious leader.

After the sons had enjoyed the feast and time together, the king appeared and approached Nic. He pointed to Nic and said, "It's time to change your clothes." I had not realized it, but he was still wearing the white and cream flowing robes that the self-righteous leaders of his former life wore. The sons at the fellowship table were all adorned with the colors of the harvest—earthy greens, bright oranges, sunshine yellows, and deep reds. The man hesitated for a moment—this robe had been the sign of his status and everything he had studied since childhood. It wasn't that he necessarily loved the robes, but they represented an integral part of his identity for many years. The robe was so essential to all of the religious leaders' identities that Nic's former peers would never even appear in public without their robes on.

As he pondered the king's request, Nic understood that the king was offering more than a fashion change. If he accepted this offer, he would permanently relinquish his identity as a religious leader from his particular region of the kingdom. Instead, he would be a son forever. I did not get to see his response that day, but, in seeing his joy in the palace, his curiosity for the new wisdom of the kingdom,[18] and his love for the king, I had no doubts as to what choice he made.

7

WORLD SYSTEMS

After participating merely as a bystander viewing these excursions from afar, I would now be granted the opportunity to experience these regions firsthand. I journeyed even farther from the palace and beyond the marketplace to a modernized city. I found myself at a house where a married couple was sitting down in their living room to watch TV after dinner. Whether I was inside the house or watching from outside, I'm not sure. In this kingdom, everything is visible, and boundaries in other kingdoms often do not apply in this one.

The husband turned on the TV to a channel displaying a man marching in place. It seemed innocent enough and looked like something one might see in a workout video. The man continued marching in place for some time, and it was apparent that he expected everyone watching to do the same thing. The couple shrugged their shoulders at each other as if to say, "Why not?" and began marching in place. Surprisingly, the two marched in perfect cadence with both the man on TV and each other. The man on TV began lifting his left arm back and forth and the couple soon followed. Then he lifted both arms, kicked a leg out, and did a 360-degree turn, all while marching in place. The couple followed in suit and mimicked each action every time, keeping in sync with the man on TV. As this progressed, the couple gave almost no thought to their actions but simply copied the man's every move because he was on TV.

After watching the couple for half an hour or so, I had the ability to see into living rooms all across the city. To my amazement, the same scenario was occurring in house after house for miles. The shows had different marching men, and each one had his own unique actions that he repeatedly performed while marching in place. In each home, the couples and families executed the precise routine of the "drill instructors."

As I stood there marveling at the sight, I then saw a massive, black machine outside the city. The machine looked like an enormous, mechanical octopus. However, rather than eight arms, it had thousands of tentacle-like cables extending out from its center. Each cable spread in different directions toward the town and connected directly into the living rooms of the houses I was watching. The people seemed to be unaware of the fact that the backs of their TVs were connected to this diabolical machine.[19] Furthermore, although I didn't see anyone operating this machine, it seemed to have a mind of its own and yielded powerful influence over what programs made it on the TVs of the town.

Because of the fact that the machine looked like a command center for evil, I could not understand why the programs appeared so innocent. In a sense, it looked like it was having a good effect on people. "At least people are getting exercise!" I thought to myself. However, I saw that once the machine had the region marching in unison with its agenda, it soon changed its approach. Night after night, it subtly introduced questionable sexual motions into its marching. However, since for weeks the people had done exactly what they saw on TV, families continued to precisely mimic what the instructors demonstrated.[20] Seeing that the morality of the programs was quickly deteriorating, I discontinued watching the disturbing sight before me.

I was curious how this machine, which seemed to so thoroughly invade the homes of this land, affected everyday life. To further investigate, I took a walk the next morning through the downtown area of the city. With its tallest building reaching only three or four stories, the city was not a major metropolitan area. However, it was clearly an affluent area and desirable to live in since it sat in a valley at the base of a beautiful mountain range.

The city possessed an intriguing dynamic as a result of the machine. In business after business and among the people walking the streets, everyone seemed to know what was happening each night in the living rooms. Yet there was little mention of what actually took place, just some occasional veiled references to let others know they were in on what was taking place nightly on television. Furthermore, the town was repulsed by the notion of guilt. Maintaining the friendly appeal of the town was of the utmost importance. People despised even the slightest hint that the machine could be negatively affecting the town.

As I walked, my eye caught a glimpse of a law office on the second floor of the building across the street from me. A lawyer was sitting in front of the window at his desk with a phone in each hand. He had a jubilant smile on his face and continued switching back and forth between the phones. I watched as he quickly picked up the phone in his right hand and briefly spoke with his wife. After about five seconds, he put down the phone in his right hand and began talking to his mistress on the phone in his left hand. He talked with her for five seconds before putting down this phone and returning to talking with his wife. After several rotations, he peered out the window and saw me watching him as I stood across the street on the sidewalk. The man knew his actions were not hidden from me and that I disapproved of his infidelity. Rather than becoming angry, he simply shrugged his shoulders and smiled at me as if to say, "Why not?" He promptly returned to alternately raising and lowering his right and left hands, each with its respective phone.

Troubled by this sight, I opted to move on and find a bite to eat. The next store down was a bakery, so I entered it to see what they had available. The store was empty except for the baker behind a glass display filled with baked goods. He greeted me, and, after talking briefly, I stepped back to decide what appealed to me on the menu. The baker didn't seem to be the type to waste time, so, when he saw I was still contemplating what to order, he turned away, apparently to attend to other duties. What proceeded next was even more disturbing than what took place in the law office.

The baker opened a small three-foot-high door behind the counter. Tucked away in this crawl space was a woman, probably in her twenties, and she was kneeling down on all fours. The baker ducked down and partially entered through the door. Immediately, they began to engage in sexual acts. I was shocked by the sadistic nature of the scene. Still in disbelief, I stepped up to order, and the baker promptly shut the door on the woman and came back to attend to me.

"How could you do that?" I wondered to myself, appalled that he would keep the woman locked away to carry about his every sexual whim.

Apparently, he could read my thoughts. "Come on, bro! Everybody's doing it," he assured me. "And, besides, she likes being here. She could leave anytime she wants, but she doesn't. She likes being here just as much as I do."

Sadly, in this particular situation, there was some truth to what he was saying. On the surface at least, the woman seemed to have no problem hiding in the crawl space and then coming out to give sexual favors when the store was not busy. From where I was standing, it also appeared that the crawl space extended to many other businesses in the town. This woman was far from being the only one in a similar position. On my journeys in the kingdom, the king would perpetually give me the perfect thing to say at the right time. However, in this case, I was speechless.

Soon, I was taken away to other sectors of the kingdom without any further instruction as I had customarily received in each town. However, I had seen enough to be broken over the depravity of this "friendly" place that by all outward appearances was an ideal city. I hoped with everything in me that someone would come after me to awaken them from their delusion or, maybe more appropriately stated, dissipation.

Sectors of Society[21]

After the bakery, I began to see various sectors of the society. I first saw the fine arts world as segments of the dance community and art community appeared before me. Without saying anything, one of the painters came up to me and said, "How dare you tell me what I can and can't do in my art!" There was a burning anger among the dancers and painters over any insinuation of right or wrong in their art.

Next, I saw the media and broadcasting segment of the society. The residents of the palace were allowed to rise up in the ranks of media and broadcasting, but this sector always kept a close watch on them. The prevailing mindset toward the sons of the king seemed to be, "You can't possibly believe that, can you!?" They tolerated the sons but viewed them as having naive mindsets that were stuck in the Dark Ages. If the sons truly took a stand and declared, "Yes, I really believe this," their coworkers began to despise them.

I then saw the world of sports and what was taking place at various stadiums, arenas, and clubhouses in this segment of the kingdom. The sons received more respect here than in any other sector in the kingdom. A curiosity about the sons prevailed in the hearts of the athletes. They couldn't figure out why the athletic sons would not join them in their questionable activities. Some of the athletes thought, "I don't understand you, so I'm not going to even try." However, some were so curious as to how the sons could live so differently that they eventually left the sports world to live in the palace.

Like the sports segment of the society, the sons of the palace had significant representation in the political arena. It seemed to make sense to me that anyone with a king for a father should have some insight into proper governing. In fact, many of the sons ventured into the political world because of their experiences in the palace. Unfortunately, many of these political sons held to the teachings of the king on secondary issues but would not represent the king on the most important political issues of their time. It seemed they often initially desired to promote what the king had taught them, but poll results among their constituents often took precedence.

The education sector was characterized by an intense drive to influence children, and "impacting the next generation" became an obsession for them. Surprisingly, most were not sure how they would influence the next generation or what specific result to aim for. However, all were steadfast in their commitment to "make a difference," even if they had no idea what that difference would be. Thus, the school teachers entered their profession utterly committed but particularly aimless in their pursuits of making a difference. I also noticed that the education sector was significantly impacted by the media sector and was intimately attached to the mechanical cords holding the society hostage.

These educators were a powerful force in the kingdom. They, like the artists, were driven by anger, yet they also had a remarkable ability to present themselves in a self-controlled manner with the appearance of dignity and peace. The artists could have had a greater effect on the kingdom, but many were too self-absorbed with their art to leave a widespread imprint on the kingdom.

Of all these sectors I visited, the sports world was the arena where the sons of the palace left the most significant mark. I was surprised by this since I had previously characterized athletes as arrogant and self-indulgent. However, I saw that their conviction arose not from the support of their fans but from fellowship with each other. Despite being one of the farthest segments of society from the palace, the fellowship present in these stadiums was almost identical to that of the palace banqueting table.

The political world seemed to be in the next best shape. The politicians gained strength from the sons of the kingdom but spent significant time worrying over the opinions of the people. Because of this, their influence for good was often sporadic or watered down.

The sons of the kingdom in the art and music world were hindered by being captive to the desires of immature sons of the king.

The musicians put out what the most immature sons demanded. Often, they huddled themselves in groups and avoided the unknown or those not associated with the palace. Some were convinced that it was impossible to influence their sector of society. Because of the widespread dysfunction across the sectors of this society, I was glad to leave this part of the kingdom.

8

FIRE AND WATER

"You must know when it is a time for fire and when it is a time for water," the king said to me. "With fire, you can take something plain and turn it into a masterpiece that the whole world marvels at. Imagine a lump of silver. As the fire heats up and the metalworker, acting as an expert silversmith, fashions it, a beautiful work of art comes forth. Intricately worked and delicately shaped, it becomes more beautiful than almost anything. Consider also an artisan teaching his son how to make weapons of war. The artisan's son curiously asks his father, 'How did this block of metal become this mighty sword?' The father answers him, 'It is by fire and only by fire that this is made possible.'

"If a soldier enters the battle with a block of iron," continued the king, "that iron will be worthless to him. Yet that exact piece of metal, mixed with fire under the guidance of a master craftsman, becomes a piercing sword. When in the hands of the trained warrior, it can strike down thousands. Through fire, the block of silver was made ready for battle. Yet who will approach the master, and who will allow him to wield his fire?

"Our enemy also comes with fire. He comes to manipulate, destroy, and burn to the ground. The same fire which is friend to the silversmith and enables his entire livelihood becomes his greatest foe when the enemy comes with fire through the hands of the arsonist. In the enemy's hands, the fire, which enabled the silversmith to purchase all his possessions, consumes all his possessions. It is at this time, when the arsonist comes, that water, not fire, is the silversmith's closest friend for it is able to save all his possessions. The enemy comes only with fire. He can only destroy and pervert. Yet the silversmith is granted both water and fire from the king, and he must discern when to use them.

"Likewise, when this metalworker goes out into the streets, he sees the beggar, addicted to drugs and destroyed by the enemy's fire. In this case, the metalworker cannot come with fire; it would overwhelm this poor man and crush his spirit. So, he comes to the beggar with a cup of cold water. The man's soul is refreshed and set free from the burning sulfur he has consumed for years."

As the king spoke, instead of just hearing his lesson, I began to see it unfold and eventually entered into the story. After giving the cup of water to the beggar, the worker passed down the street and eventually came upon a group of four finely dressed, rich, young men who had just gotten off work. Confident and full of success stories, they would daily share their professional feats with one another. The men lived only half a block from the beggar yet knew nothing of the man, nor did they care about his misery.

The metalworker, who I had learned was one of the king's sons, approached the men knowing his water was of little use and would not be accepted by them. On the other hand, a metalworker who had good intentions but was immature would have offered the men the water anyway. Since the men had plenty of money and all life's necessities, they would have laughed at the metalworker's offer of free water, saying, "We've been drinking all day. We don't need your water!" The water that the immature worker was offering was of a different nature than anything they had ever tasted, of course, but the men would have no knowledge of this, for they saw no need for the water.

Recognizing this, a wise metalworker would have known that this was not the time to offer the cold cup of water that had gloriously transformed the beggar on the street half a block away. He also would know that this was not the time to bring one of his finest swords and strike the men down. So, instead, the wise metalworker presented the men with fire.

I watched intently as the wise metalworker approached the men. Since I had seen people give water to beggars but had never seen anyone give fire to a group of young professionals, I was eager to see their reaction. From overhearing their conversation, I learned the professions of three of them: One was a successful businessman, one was a lawyer, and one was a politician. They were standing in front of the steps of a large state capitol building, which was next door to the business office and the law firm.

As he approached the men, the metalworker's heart filled with a fiery, liquid gold. It began bubbling up from his heart and out of his mouth. As he spoke to the men, the fiery gold began flowing out of his mouth. Having never seen anything like this before, the men were caught completely by surprise. Furthermore, in all their years in the upper echelons of business, law, and politics, they had never heard words spoken with such authority.

In between staring at the worker in amazement, they would sneak glances at each other trying to catch a glimpse of one another's reactions. They would have normally been too embarrassed to pay any attention to some guy on the street, but, again, they had never witnessed anything like this. As confident as the four men were in their respective lines of work, each had spent his entire life laboring for the praise of his peers. None of the four wanted to be caught being tricked by this street preacher.

The liquid, fiery gold continued to pour forth from the metalworker's mouth and began piercing like arrows the hearts of the four men. Still in shock, one of the men asked the others, "Brothers, what should we do?" When the man spoke, the fire ceased flowing from the metalworker's mouth. Despite knowing the answer to the man's question, he knew that this was not time to provide answers but to let them come to their own conclusions.

"We must repent," was the unanimous response of the four men. So, right in front of the business, the law firm, and the capitol to which they had given their entire adult lives, they knelt down on the sidewalk. They began repenting for their pride, their greed, and a litany of other shortcomings. As they did this, the fiery gold began to flow again, not in the mouth of the metalworker but in a single streak that flowed through and connected each man's heart.

It was then—and not until then—that the master metalworker pulled out the cup of cold water from the king's table. Upon seeing it, the men begged, "Yes, please give us this water. We're burning up inside!" The cup had always been an elaborately decorated chalice, but the four were not able to recognize it as such until the liquid fire flowed through their hearts. Like the beggar earlier, they each drank and were deeply refreshed by this new water. Surprisingly, the water did not extinguish the fire. Instead, it enabled the men to handle the fire. Rather than consume them, the fire began cleansing their entire beings and filling them with power. The metalworker had seen this process before, but he was used to seeing metal, not men, refined in the fire.

"Come on," the metalworker said, "I have bread to give you, too." As he began to lead the men to the palace, I noticed that the palace was very close to the political building, law offices, and businesses. In fact, from the steps you could actually see the dome of the palace. Yet, despite the close proximity of the political, law, and business structures, the men had never been aware of the location of the palace. In all the years of their most important transactions and decisions, they had never sought the nearby palace or king for direction. As they continued on their journey, following the worker to the palace, I questioned if their visit to the palace was premature. But I reasoned, "They *have to* meet the king."

Along the way, the metalworker received word from the king that the men were to go straight to his throne room. In a few minutes, the metalworker and four men reached the palace steps. As they were about to ascend the steps, the metalworker was about to stop and ask if they truly wanted to go in. It seemed that even he was caught off guard by how rapidly the events had progressed. Despite the liquid fire that flowed through the men's hearts and the dramatic change in their attitudes, the metalworker still wanted to make sure they were not just getting caught up in the emotion of the situation.

The metalworker was also pondering if they had the *right* to go straight to the throne room. After all, many had spent years, or in my case months, waiting outside the palace before they entered to the throne room. For whatever reason, people rarely immediately entered the throne room when they arrived at the palace. Also, sons of the king stopped many visitors at the steps. These sons inhibited the new visitors by telling them that in order to enter the throne room they needed to learn and memorize many facts about the history of the palace and the famous battles fought in the land. In addition, because of these sons' obsession with trivia questions, they required newcomers to answer trivia about the king in order to enter the palace.[22]

After I watched the metalworker lead them, I was again shown a potential scenario of how an immature metalworker would have responded to these men. I saw the immature metalworker first try to convince the professionals that fire really had flown through his mouth to each of their hearts. He also repeatedly questioned them to ensure that they did not doubt the king's existence. He also asked them to meet weekly with him in front of the palace for two years to discuss the king. He did this to make sure they really were ready to meet the king. Even after the two years were completed, the immature metalworker still thought in the back of his mind that they may not be ready to meet the king. It seemed after two years of work, he was less convinced they were fit to see the king than the mature metalworker was after five minutes with the men.

I drifted back to the events taking place before me. The master metalworker knew that he could not hesitate in following the king's command. Each man was a blank slate in regards to the things of the palace; they followed whatever example the metalworker set. Because the metalworker took them straight to the king, the men assumed this was standard palace procedure.[23] He turned to boldly walk up the stairs, and, in turn, the four men followed with the same measure of confidence. They went right through the palace door, through the war corridor, and into the throne room. They walked across the massive red carpet and knelt on the steps by the throne.

I greatly enjoyed seeing the hearts and attitudes of these four men. Everyone in the palace loved seeing those visiting the king for the first time. Behaving like little children, everything was exciting to them. Of course, we were always a little convicted by their passion for the king and the experiences in the palace, but we didn't mind. It was good for us.

The first man was bowing on the steps in amazement. "I can't believe this is really true!" he said to himself. One by one, the memories of his life unfolded in his mind. All the fragmented pieces that had brought so much confusion began to make sense. He could see in situation after situation how the king had been personally involved in his life even though he was unaware of the king's company at the time. So many life events worked out that shouldn't have. Other times, he somehow knew exactly what to do in situations but refused and reaped the consequences of his wrong choices. Numerous friends had referenced the king in conversations, but he was oblivious to the significance of their comments. He now recognized all of these as the presence of the king in his life. He was almost laughing at himself, thinking, "How could I have missed *so much* and not been aware of the king?!" There had even been a season when he confidently declared to others, "There is no king!" However, he now sat astonished and amazed at how active the king had been throughout his lifetime.

The second man was weeping as he also reflected on the events of his life. Over and over he asked himself, "How could I have been so stubborn? How could I have been so foolish?" He was thinking in particular about the worthlessness of the pursuits to which he had devoted his adult years. It was as if the building blocks of his life, his priorities, and his motives were being dramatically rearranged in just a few minutes. Recollections of striving for promotions, milestones, and empty life benchmarks continued to consume his thoughts as he wept and shook his head. While many things come to light in the presence of the king, motives of the heart are always one of the first things to be revealed.

In a similar fashion to the first two, the third man was clearly reflecting on his past with a new perspective. Then, I looked over to the fourth man and saw that he was struggling. An unhealthy sense of self-awareness seemed to grip him. He was unsure of how to act and respond around the king. His thoughts drifted to his job back at the office. (I now knew this man was also a business professional.) This recently discovered reality of the presence of the king did not seem compatible with his former life. "How would people at work respond if he spoke of the king?" Just thinking about the conversations that could ensue was awkward for him. On the other hand, if he was to live with the king, how could he give himself fully to his job, knowing that his business pursuits paled in comparison to the priorities of the palace? Furthermore, the ways of the palace, which he was quickly learning, did not seem to mesh with some of the business objectives of his company. It simply did not seem fair to his partners who had worked for years toward a common goal to introduce an entirely new set of objectives.

As soon as the fourth man began valuing the king only in relation to how he benefited the man's career, things inside of him became darker. After a few minutes, a group of mockingbirds with pointed beaks flew at the man and encircled him. They were full of accusations, which they continually whispered in his ears. I knew that they were sent by the enemy and was surprised that they could even enter the palace, let alone the throne room. Unfortunately, these mockingbirds were skilled at completing their assignment.

After thinking about office life for a while, the man also began reflecting on his childhood. Yet, with the mockingbirds present, the response to the memories was markedly different than his three friends' responses to their own reminiscing on their lives. Like them, he saw instances of the king's presence in his life, but he viewed these encounters as uninvited intrusions into his life and career pursuits.

He began to yell at the king, "How dare you demand me and everyone in this kingdom to follow all your rules! What right do you have to force your rules upon us?" He could have come up with many more accusations but voiced the ones that most annoyed him. Because of the man's skewed perceptions of the king, the man resented that the king would sit in his cozy and richly ornamented palace while people in the real world were out struggling to survive. This presumed indifference of the king angered him, but the demand that all the king's rules be followed irked him the most. After several minutes of internally ranting, he was interrupted by a thought, "You're not allowed to get mad at the king. He is always right." However, the man justified his anger and presumptions with the notion that the king had no idea what he endured daily in order to succeed at work. He thought to himself, "There are just certain things that people don't understand that have to be done in the business world."

Through all of this, the king had not said a word to the four men. Of course, the king, like the rest of us watching, could perceive the thoughts and intentions of each man. In the midst of the first three men's personal encounters with the king, the three men were simultaneously mindful of the internal conflict of the fourth man. I, along with the three men, was surprised that with all his doubts and accusations, he did not simply get up and leave the premises. Yet a lingering, internal compulsion kept him from taking off for the door. I glanced over at the other three who now had transitioned their own personal reminiscing to fully focusing on the fluctuating condition of the fourth man. In the midst of their concern, each began speaking things to the king about their friend in languages that I didn't understand.

This scene—the fourth man deciding if he would stay or leave, the friends talking to the king about him, and the king waiting patiently—remained fixed before me for several days. After days of internal wrestling, the man decided that he would return to his former life. He promptly declared his intentions to the king, who in turn invited the man to a series of exit meetings. The three other men were crushed by their friend's decision and couldn't believe he desired to return to the life that they were so relieved to leave behind.

"Why couldn't we change his heart?" they asked the king when the fourth man exited the room. They thought that after all their time talking with the king about their friend he would decide to stay.

I knew the king was pleased that the men had approached him to discuss their friend's situation. He affirmed them by saying, "My sons, I have not called you to change his heart but rather to be faithful to do what I ask you to do." Even though these men were new to the palace, I could relate to their struggle. They were already wrestling with questions and concerns that long-term residents of the palace agonized over.

The king and the fourth man began to meet each day and talk about his return to his previous life. They would walk down the corridor, much like the king walked with Nic and discussed the implications of the reality of the kingdom upon Nic's arrival. The two took long strolls discussing the details and the timing of the man's departure. It was a solemn sight to see, and one that broke my heart to watch. Despite not knowing this man, I felt his friends' pain over him willfully rejecting the king. I believe the whole palace was grieved over this one man.

I have pondered for many years[24] over the method in which this man left the palace. I'm still not sure what it was that kept him from getting up and walking away the moment his attitude toward the king changed. The prolonged discussions—not with the people of the palace or those in the courtyard but with the king himself—were a mystery to me. Leaving the king and his palace was far more calculated and meticulous than I had imagined. The man knew what he was doing.

Eventually, the day for his departure came. I saw the pain in the king's face as the man prepared to leave. "What kind of king is this?" I wondered. "Who would care so much for someone who daily threatened, 'I'm leaving you'?"

The man returned to his former life and rejoined his company. He did not chase after the career goals or promotions with his previous fervor. As a result of simply spending a brief time in the throne room, his perspective and priorities had changed. The achievements for which he worked sixteen-hour, anxiety-filled days now seemed not worth his time. His demeanor and interactions with employees became more relaxed. He had a new sense of what was worth the effort and a keen awareness of how to more efficiently accomplish tasks. He worked less and accomplished more. Because of his transformation at the palace, it became a joke at the company that those who were constantly stressing out and making their coworkers miserable should go spend a few weeks at the "imaginary palace."

As the man continued to ascend in the business world, his focus shifted to equipping the next generation of business leaders. He managed his department by motivating the young men to direct all their energy to climbing the corporate ladder. Since they worked for him, he typically received the credit for the fruits of their labor. Eventually, they would be so burned out that they would run to him for counsel for both their careers and personal lives. As a result, these employees became entirely dependent upon him. In their vulnerable states, the man would offer them his secrets to success. Consequently, their esteem for him continued to elevate.

Through his "helping" the next generation, the man grew increasingly arrogant. He regularly commended himself for resting more while producing better returns by benefiting from the labor of others. Employees became captive to his arrogance and craved his approval. Other directors at the company concealed their jealousy in order to remain on his good side.

The successful businessman especially enjoyed when a son of the palace came to work for his company. "I know exactly how they think," he thought and took great delight in relying on his experience with the palace to direct these sons in the way he wanted them to go. All the new employees didn't know it, but the man was an expert at sounding like he was on their side all the while using them for the sake of his own agendas. Even though other managers sometimes did not understand the sons of the king and even feared them, this man not only understood how they thought but he also was an expert at *changing* how they thought.

His plan was calculated and effective. When a new son of the king would come, he would immediately support and encourage the new hire. Soon, he would begin to talk of promotion not in terms of greater riches and accolades but in terms of influence within the company. It was speaking of "influence within the company" that especially hooked the young ones. In the name of future influence, the new employees poured themselves into their work and began working far more hours than they had ever intended. Eventually, the sons would mostly forget why the king sent them from the palace into business in the first place. The man had no greater joy than knowing that he had caused the sons of the palace to forget the king. Although he had done many things against the king, this was his greatest fault and the one for which he would be most severely punished one day. Through all of this, he knew in the back of his mind that the king knew what he was doing—he simply did not think the king would ever do anything about it.

9

SETTING OUT TO FIGHT

The three friends who had not left the palace were still in the same position on their knees before the throne. They arose and began walking towards the fellowship hall. I assumed that they were getting ready to eat the bread the metalworker had promised them, but I sensed that the king did not plan on feeding them. I asked the king, "What about the bread that the metalworker promised them?" The king had already gone ahead of us. When we caught up with him, he was whispering to someone behind a door in the hallway. Their conversation was about something very solemn and private, and we had to wait a long time for them to finish their serious discourse. I wanted to peek behind the door to see who he was talking with, but I knew he simply wanted me to wait. During this time, I had noticed that, as the men walked toward the fellowship hall, full body metal armor had formed on them. I had a sense that they were preparing for battle rather than a feast. The training grounds were just on the other side of the fellowship hall. Because of the breadth of what we had all learned in the fellowship hall, I thought, "It's not right to send them to battle when they haven't eaten yet."

After a long wait for the king to finish his pressing conversation, he turned to me and said, "You will lead them." By "lead them," the king meant that I would lead them in battle. As always, he would be with me and guide me, although I would not be able to see him at all times. Furthermore, the men understood that since the king had appointed me to lead them, to follow me would be to follow him. As we walked out of the palace and beyond the training yards, we approached a battlefield. I began to ponder the apparent paradox that I had trained for many years for this battle, yet these men had in no way been trained or even shared in the fellowship meal. However, I knew that if the king was calling us to this battle, this was one we could win. He assured me that it was not necessary for them to have passed through the training grounds to be successful.

I began to think that if these men could win victories with no training at all maybe my various exercises in jousting, sword fighting, and the other drills were unnecessary. The king responded by laying out several potential battle scenarios before my eyes. He showed me an army who had freshly encountered the king but had not yet had any further training. These passionate, courageous, rookie soldiers stormed the battlefield, and they let out an echoing battle cry as they charged. Mostly by sheer courage and zeal, they pushed back the enemy and sent those troops fleeing. The new army won several consecutive victories as the enemy was not accustomed to encountering such passion. However, eventually, the enemy forces grew wise and realized that the king's army was operating solely on passion and was devoid of discernment or any concrete strategy. The enemy divided forces and set ambushes in front of and behind the rookie army. Because the army drove the enemy forces back so far, their passion blinded them from seeing that they were working their way into the enemy's devastating trap. As imminent destruction loomed, the king prevented me from seeing the end of the battle. I was glad I didn't have to witness the carnage but knew that those types of battles were not always cut short before the troops were slaughtered.

I then inquired of the king as to how an army that had been solely composed of those equipped in the training grounds would fare. I then watched as a mass of them left the training ground and entered the battlefield. They did not charge right away at the enemy as the previous army had. They were confident that with their excellent training they could soundly defeat an attacking enemy. As they patiently waited, they discussed techniques from their training days. They began demonstrating to one another various offensive positions, swipes with their swords, and blocks with their shields. As they did this, they were able to sharpen one another as each one taught skills that those around them had not yet acquired. During this process, their confidence continued to grow so that they could defeat any army that threatened them.

Meanwhile, the enemy realized that the king's army was not attacking. They too had patience to wait. They had already won many victories to get this far. The enemy generals were more than happy to give their troops a break as well as some time to savor the victories on the fields behind them.

I could see that, after a while, the king's army made a small attack and then began declaring victory. They had entered into battle after years of training and had not lost a single soldier. As we viewed this sight, the king, with his heart clearly grieved, turned to me and said, "This could have been a great victory. These men were well trained to defeat this army and drive them back while inflicting significant losses on the enemy. They could have driven them back as far as the army of those who had freshly encountered the king and been completely prepared to fend off any ensuing ambush. In my eyes, because this should have been a great victory, this was a great defeat."

Through these two scenarios, I learned that the king usually desired armies consisting of the wisdom of seasoned warriors and the zeal of new recruits.

People of the Land

After the king had notified me that I would lead this new army of four, we took with us the armor and swords that we would need for the fight. I did not yet know our mission or destination, so we just started walking. We did not head straight to the middle of the battlefield where the previous fights had taken place. Instead, we walked along the right side of the battlefield. After walking for a long time, we encountered a family gathered around a campfire and cooking a meal for dinner. They were friendly and did not seem to be intimidated by four men dressed for battle intruding on their family dinner. I asked the father, who spoke with a Spanish accent and had a large sombrero, if he was for or against the king.

"We are neither for nor against the king," he responded. "We just want to live in peace on this plot of land that our forefathers gave us. Here, my family can grow, and eat, and enjoy each other."

"So you don't know the king, do you?"

"We know there is a king in this land. He does not seem very real to us, though, because we have never seen him or met him. Yet, we know he exists because our forefathers many generations ago knew the king and put their hope in the king. To this day, we still have the stories they passed on. We trust our forefathers, and they trusted in the king—or at least that the king would one day come for them—so, because of this, we have hope that there is a king somewhere."

"Everyone is either for or against the king,"[25] I explained, "Even if you have never met him."

I was struggling with what to do as I talked with the family. I did not know if it was wiser to take them along with us to provide on the spot training for them or if I should send them back to meet the king. I decided to ask the king. (On the battlefield, anyone could still talk and listen to him from his tower, even if he was far away from the fight.) He simply told me to make the decision that I thought was best. I decided to take the same approach the king had just taken with me; so, I asked the men what we should do.

"We would want to go meet the king first," they responded. I knew this was the correct response. I realized part of my motivation for wanting them to go with us was because I was concerned about the size of my army. After all, I had never seen a four-person army win a great battle. Upon realizing I was more concerned about me than them, I asked the father, "Would you like to go meet the king now?"

He looked at his family as they ate their meal. I was a little embarrassed asking him this since I had just met him and was asking him to travel away from his lot of land that he had lived on his whole life.

The father apparently could read my mind and responded, "Although our forefathers passed this land down to us, I am ready to leave it to take my family to meet the king. This land has been in our family line for many generations, but all we have is this little area around the campfire."

My three companions and I looked at each other surprised as if to say, "An invitation so simple would have never convinced me!"

I was surprised that this man was so quick to pack up his family and take them to a foreign land. He seemed to not think much about it. He simply thought that since we carried ourselves with authority and since the only purpose he had had for many years was to eat around the campfire with his family every night, he might as well go. There was no dramatic fiery encounter as these three former professionals had experienced, simply an offer of purpose to a family that didn't have one.

As the family arose to leave, the man added, "And, besides, this king was the hope of my forefathers."

I sent one of my men to lead the family to the palace to meet the king. As he came near the palace, my comrade was filled with a dynamic excitement. He remembered his anticipation and joy on the first day he approached the king's palace. Now, in the same way, he was happy not just for himself but also for the family. There is a special contentment for every true son of the kingdom in seeing someone come to the palace for the first time.

10

THE OLD WEST

After a few days, our companion returned to us, and we continued on from the campground. The men and I recognized that in the region beyond the battlefield there was an invisible line that divided the area into two sections—the enemy's side and the king's side. As we ventured onward, it was unclear which side of the battlefield we were on since we were so far away from the battlefield. We eventually came upon a town that looked like a town from the American Old West in the 1800's. Saloons, small shops, and places to tie horses lined the center of town. Furthermore, the population of this town was comprised entirely of homosexuals. Soon, all the men came out to meet us in the village square. There looked to be several hundred of them forming a semicircle in front of us. We could tell they were interested in talking to us, and there was no apparent hostility among them.

"Do you come here to stab us with your swords?" a man who stepped up from the middle of the group asked me. I realized that we were dressed in chain mail and carrying majestic swords, which did not seem to be the best approach to peacefully enter a town.

"Many have tried to before. It won't work," he continued. At this, he grabbed a wooden sword and began to stab himself through the heart. The sword pierced his heart and came out of his back. Men all over began grabbing flimsy wooden swords which were pitiful in comparison to the long, shining metal swords with which we were equipped. They all began stabbing themselves through the heart with these wooden swords in a mechanical, back-and-forth motion. To say the least, my company and I were shocked, not understanding exactly what was happening or why being stabbed did not hurt them.

"We did not come here to fight you," I answered.

"Then what did you come here for?" asked the same man, obviously the leader of the people.

I did not know exactly why we were there. We had simply been traveling and had come upon this town. However, I knew the king wanted us to meet these people.

"We come in the name of the king," I responded in a loud voice so all could hear.

There were many reactions to this statement. Some laughed; some were curious; some seemed to be filled with a deep longing; and some were angry. The leader did not have much of a reaction to my statement. He clearly had been in contact with sons of the king before. My guess is that the town nominated him as the leader because of his ability to keep his emotions in check and remain calm and collected.

"Do you intend to rule over us?" he asked me, rather incredulously, "Because it won't work. Many have come and tried to rule over us and set up laws in order to exercise authority over us. These people won't follow an outsider. They're not interested in a foreigner coming to our city and telling us to obey a system of rules where the outsider is the originator and ultimate interpreter of the law."

"No, we don't come to exercise authority over you," I answered.

"Then tell us why you're here," he said.

As we were talking, I could see that there were three main types of people in this crowd. The first, which was the majority of them, viewed the king in direct relation to past encounters they had with sons of the king. Their minds' image of him was almost totally shaped by encounters with the first two or three people they had met who claimed to be the king's sons. The second group, a smaller portion of the people, espoused to not like the sons of the king, but, nevertheless, they still believed in their hearts that the king was better and more kind than those they had met who claimed to be the king's sons. They clung to a hope in their hearts that one day they would be granted an opportunity to meet the king, and they had told other people in the town about their hope. It seemed as if most of the town did not know how to respond to this group. Their image of the king was tainted by experiences with sons they had met. However, the innocence of the sliver of hope of their friends was contagious. The final group was the smallest but most influential. They saw past the sons of the king and saw what the king was really like, and they deeply resented him. While only composing about ten percent of the people, their influence was immense and seemed to have affected all but ten percent of the town.

My thoughts drifted back to the leader's question which I had still not answered. I had not responded to him simply because I did not know the answer myself. Without any forethought, I called out, "We come because the king desires sons." When I heard that come out of my mouth, I quickly realized this was the right answer.

"Your king is a hypocrite and a father of hypocrites," a man a few rows back shouted. There was a mixture of rage and pain in his voice as he yelled this. Many others began to join in the accusations. The men were shouting different things at us. Others were yelling just to yell. Still others were arguing with each other about their interpretations of the king and their opinions of the sons of the king. The vastly different experiences in their encounters with the sons of the king were definitely a source of confusion in this town.

I could see that the leader did not fully agree with this statement, and that he wanted to calm the townspeople. Unfortunately, he could not come up with a response to counter this statement and was thus left unsure about what to do or how to prevent a riot.

"Friends," I called out, trying to shout over the hundreds of voices clamoring all at once, "Please come join us tonight for dinner!" Once again, words had slipped out of my mouth before I had the opportunity to mentally process them. It was as if the king's chief counselor, Suelo, who had taught me in the training grounds, was right there with me, giving the exact answers I needed at the right time.

The crowd was as caught off guard as I was at this response and did not know how to answer. Our invitation did, however, have a calming effect on the people, and it seemed like a good proposition to the leader and the rest of the people.

"So we will have dinner tonight with them," I thought to myself, surprised at how things had developed.

Later that night, we all dined at a large, 1850s-style saloon. Everyone sat at one table that wrapped around the room. We all enjoyed the meal and casually talked among ourselves. The man who had yelled at us about the hypocrisy of our king was sitting across the table from me. He was now a little ashamed of what he had done, especially since we had shown generosity to the town by inviting them to eat with us. The man explained that he was not an outgoing person and was typically reserved. However, this normally timid man was fed up with people coming to their town and starting arguments just to tell them they were wrong. The reason for his outburst today was that he had grown increasingly angry with men in the town who would not speak up for themselves. Our gentle response to his outburst had clearly softened his heart to some degree.

As dinner proceeded, there seemed to be a growing anticipation among the crowd that we had something to say to them. Through our conversation earlier in the day, they discovered what we were *not* here to do but were still wondering what we *were* here to do. I sensed this expectation, and the king (remember, he is always there to lead his sons) showed me an approach *not* to take. I received that it would not be effective to flatter them along the lines of, "The king loves you so much and thinks you're great. He thinks you're all really special." They would feel patronized by this and other similar statements. We entered their town clothed in chain mail and swords and ready to fight a battle. They all knew we were on a mission, and they were eager to know its purpose.

I stood up to address all the men, again not knowing what would come out of my mouth.

"The king desires sons," I declared. "Most kings desire their people to obey them, to honor them, to live in peace, and to not cause trouble. They want things to go smoothly for them, and they want to be liked by the people, but that is the extent of the relationship. Kings don't go around trying to adopt all their people! But our king is different, brothers. Our king is unlike any other king. He is after sons. He wants sons. And he desires that every one of you in this room would become his son. This is why we are here, friends, and this is our message to you."

The whole room listened intently. Even though I had mentioned a similar sentiment earlier in the day, this was now striking a deep chord within them. They had not heard someone speak with such authority, at least not authority that was reinforced by love for them. I had the attention of the eyes and the hearts of everyone.

"The king desires that everyone who wants to be his son come with me right now. Do not hesitate, brothers! Everyone who wishes to be a son of the king, meet me outside!"

This was another case of personally feeling uncomfortable with my own words. Not understanding the logic behind what I was saying, I still knew my declarations came straight from the king. However, my natural mind reasoned that this approach was too abrupt and would send the message that we were eager to abandon them and our budding friendships. Also, I feared the town would be very angry that we had marched in and immediately took some of their people away.

Not knowing if any would join us, the four of us went outside into the town square. More people than we expected followed us outside the saloon. The full moon above was our only source of light as about thirty men circled around us. They were eagerly waiting to hear what we would say next. While many came, there were still more inside that had been gripped by my words but simply were not willing or ready to take definitive action.

On my right I saw a pretty, young Asian woman whose heart seemed very pure as she waited for me to speak. "So there *are* women here!" I thought to myself. I had wondered if there were only men in this town. I hadn't seen any women earlier, but, as I learned on the training grounds, there are always many things going on around us that we don't even notice.

"Let's get going," I said to the crowd. I did not know how we would get all these people to the palace and did not want to take the chance of them getting lost along the way. As I looked down the road, I saw the palace on the horizon. I didn't know how it was so near this Old Western town because it had taken us days to arrive here. However, somehow in the kingdom, the moment these people wanted to meet the king, the palace was nearby. Suelo told me that, with the exception of three individuals, we should send all of the consenting townspeople straight to the palace. The three who remained behind would join our group and continue on our mission with us.

Without a huge pep talk or any chance for them to go back to their homes to get belongings, they set out straight for the palace.[26]

"Do not turn back or stop 'til you reach the palace!" I urged them.

As the group ventured northeast toward the palace, the seven of us continued north on our journey. As I mentioned before, it is always a great joy to see people come to the palace for the first time. Even though we did not accompany them to the palace, the king opened our eyes to see what was happening with a few of the new sons and daughters. They did not go to the training grounds or to the fellowship table to eat but simply spent their days individually walking with and getting to know the king. (Remember, while not possible in our world, in the kingdom it is possible for many to simultaneously spend all day individually with the king.)

At our distance, I continued to watch as the king took some of the men to different places in his palace, including a lounge area and the bedroom. He would take them to places and situations very similar to experiences they had when they were younger. As youth, some of these men in a similar scenario had been manipulated and taken advantage of by older men. There were deep scars and areas of sensitivity related to these events. Yet, the king deliberately had furniture with similar set ups and sat with the men in ways that paralleled the events leading up to when these men had their trust betrayed and bodies violated at a young age. As this happened, the memories aroused in the men caused uncertainty and fear. Yet, as they came to find out, the king did not take advantage of their weaknesses. He was not driven by sexuality or by a desire to prey on others' vulnerabilities. He was driven by love. In this way, he redeemed not only these men's futures but also their pasts, ones that had haunted them since youth.

One day, I saw the king interacting with one of the women. She had spent years training herself to be as masculine as possible. I incorrectly assumed the king would immediately try to make the woman feel and be feminine. The king's ways were very different. He did not require her to wear a pretty, pink dress and ask everyone to look at her and say how beautiful she was. This would have only made her feel uncomfortable. Instead, he walked with her and listened to her as she progressively confided in him about her life experiences. He was very gentle with her and did not force his ways upon her. When the women opened up about painful subjects or lies she believed, the king was quick to replace lies with truth and reveal her true identity.

The approach the king took in courting her, introducing her to himself and to his court, was in some ways similar to how her long-term girlfriend had pursued her. The girlfriend, who was not at the palace, had been involved in homosexuality for several years when the two met. Because of this, she slowly led the woman through the ins and outs of a relationship. Also, when the woman had shared with her girlfriend about painful experiences, the girlfriend would always respond with, "That's exactly what happened to me," or "I know exactly how you feel." In this way, they drew close to one another because of their mutual experiences while also often uniting through channeling their bitterness in a common direction. To this woman, even though the king was a man, he was someone she could share her life with and relate to intimately. The king spent many hours with the woman listening to her share her memories, many of which were painful and difficult to express. Though she didn't know it at the time, the king had been there and seen each moment. Still, he would patiently listen to her and then speak truth about what had taken place and why those experiences did not define her. In this way, the king formed a deep bond of love and trust between him and the woman.

Comparing her time with the king with her experiences with her former girlfriend, the woman explained, "She told me I was not the only one, and so I trusted her." The woman continued, "On the other hand, the king told me I *was* the only one,[27] that there's no one else like me, and, because of this, he loves me.[28] She told me to which community I belonged. The king told me who I am, and, because of who I am to him, I belong. Before, my identity was based on what had happened to me. Now, my identity is based on who I was made to be."

The relationship between the woman and the king went beyond just her opening up to him. She had opened up to people before. Now, though, she was able to understand, accept, and love herself for who she was.

I also watched how the king courted—introduced to himself and his court—the man. He did not immediately try to make the man engage in activities perceived to be manly or macho. Instead, the king focused on the man simply being with him. And, as activities such as archery or swordsmanship arose in the king's schedule, he included the man in what he was doing. While working and doing things together, the man opened up to the king, and the king spoke truth about who the man was and his past experiences. The revelation of the man's true identity happened gradually and naturally.

The man had never known such a deep fulfillment in his entire life: He had a true father for the first time. He expressed, "Every boy wants to be like his dad. He wants his dad to take him places and include him in what he's doing. I liked when my dad was interested in what was important to me and *what I was doing*, but, more importantly, I wanted my dad to include me in what *he was doing*. I wanted my dad to think I was good enough and strong enough to come with him when he was playing sports or doing difficult tasks. The king has done this for me, and, because of this, I love him with all my heart. He is the father I always wished I had."

11

EBONY

Traveling onward, we came across a present-day, small, semi-urban town. This town was also far away from the battlefield, and we were uncertain as to which side of the battlefield we were on. I entered the town and saw that everyone in the town was Black. Unlike the previous town, we did not have a crowd of citizens waiting for us upon our arrival. Instead, people were scattered throughout the town in different locations.

As I walked into the town, a large Black woman in her mid-thirties greeted me. Her weathered face and skin conveyed that she had endured life experiences beyond her years. She had a red bandana around her head and appeared to be knitting something as she sat. The woman was a single mother and had several small children around her.

"How you boys doing?" she asked.

"We're doing fine," I replied. I wasted no time and got right to the point by quickly adding, "We are here to help."

"Every time you folk come around here, you try to help us. But all you focus on is how I made a mistake and ended up with these kids. Why can't you treat them like real children instead of just talking about my mistake?"

"Yes, but how many times did you make that mistake?" I questioned her.

"Boy, what the h--- is wrong with you!? That's exactly what I'm talking about! My babies need food. They need education. They need a *father*, and all you do is try to make me feel guilty all the time."

I cut her off with a rhetorical question.

"Where *are* the fathers in this place?" I asked.

I wasn't interested in her excuses. I walked away and went looking to see if there were any fathers or husbands in this town. Walking deeper into the town, we came across six or seven men sitting down on the side of a road across from a park with a basketball court.

"What's going on, bro?" one of the men greeted me, as he did a multi-step handshake with his right hand and gave me a pat on the back with the left. Both he and the previous woman were, initially, surprisingly welcoming.

Judging by the sun, it was around noon. The men were all sweating in the hot weather.

"Don't you guys have work to be doing?" I asked them.

"Man we've been working hard all day," one of them said.

"Playing basketball doesn't count as work," I shot back.

"Man, who the h--- you think you are, coming in here and telling us how to live?"

"I'm just speaking the truth. Don't get mad at me because of your laziness," I told them.

At this, they all stood up to fight me. However, because I walked in power as a son of the king, I struck them with blindness.[29] My friends and I walked right past them as they groped about, suddenly in a daze. I noticed some of my men had been uneasy with my comments. I was okay with this. I knew they needed to learn about tough love. Also, they had seen how much the king esteemed me and had seen some of the battles I had won. They had learned to trust me.

I soon found a well-equipped office where I could relax and refocus my mind. The office appeared as if someone had set it up just for me. It had hardwood floors, a cherry wood desk, and a comfortable, black reclining chair. Most importantly, on this especially hot day, the office was air conditioned.

"I just need to plan so I can figure out how to fix this town," I said to myself. I eagerly went to work strategizing and forming programs and policies for these people. Like an expert architect, I mapped out after-school programs, parenting classes, feeding centers, job training schools, and other essentials for restoring this town.

As I was planning, a beautiful, light-skinned Black woman walked by my window. I noticed she seemed to shoot a quick smile in my direction. Her walk and gaze played through my mind in slow motion. I was caught off guard by her beauty. I jumped up and headed toward the door to meet her. As I passed my desk, I stopped myself thinking, "I'm a spiritual leader. My followers can't see me flirting with a woman."

"No," I told myself, "I'm not going to avoid talking with her just because she's pretty. I won't lust over her. I'll just enjoy her beauty and have a quick chat. Then I can get back to work."

The woman and I talked for a little while. She was very charming, and we did not end up talking about anything important. I was fine with the small talk since I was just looking to enjoy her beauty for a little and was feeling affirmed since she was paying me attention. It was apparent that she was flirting with me some, but I reasoned this was okay since I was not here to control every detail of how other people should act. I just had to make sure I wasn't flirting with her, at least not in a noticeable way, in case one of the men returned and witnessed my actions. We said goodbye. She gave me one last smile and then walked away.

"No harm done," I thought to myself. "Now I need to get back to planning so I can figure out how to get this town to where it should be."

I worked well into the night writing, planning, and diagramming a road map to success for the town. If they would just listen to me and be willing to change their thought patterns and habits, this could be an entirely new community.

It was getting late, and I began to think of my men. I wasn't sure where they were, but I knew that they might have some questions since they were a little uneasy with my behavior earlier in the day.

As I reviewed the day in my mind, I too became slightly concerned about some of my actions. A lengthy internal dialogue ensued as I vacillated between feeling convicted for my actions and attempting to justify them.

"Why did I try to make the woman feel guilty?"

"Because she wasn't admitting that she had done wrong and was putting the blame on us," I reasoned.

"Why did I view her children as less important?"

"Because they all came from different men and their mother was irresponsible."

"Should this matter as to how much value the child has?"

"And why was I so upset at the men sitting by the park?"

"Because their laziness and unfaithfulness is what got this town into this mess in the first place."

"But do you know for sure that these men had done this?"

"No, but I wouldn't be surprised if they had."

As I sat alone with my thoughts, my focus turned toward my motivation and intentions for my comments. I was surprised at how quickly my heart had grown calloused. There were a number of hidden judgments in my heart that I did not even know were present. I had never vocalized any animosity toward Blacks and had always discouraged those who did. Where was this coming from?[30]

I wondered what the men had thought. I assumed at the time they would just trust me since they had seen me walk in great wisdom and win several battles in just a short time. After all, I was not self-appointed; it was the king who appointed me. I gradually realized the king was right there in the office with me. I'm not sure how it's possible to gradually realize someone is standing in the room with you, but things are like that in this kingdom. The more convicted I became regarding my actions, the more I was aware he was there.

"Many people expect others to follow them because of past victories," the king told me.[31] "They did great things for me several years back and won the attention of many. These memories become the basis for their confidence to lead as well as their assurance that people will continue to follow them. The people continue to follow even when the leader behaves questionably because they think, 'Remember how he did that amazing thing back then? He has to be sent from the king.' So they continue to follow without questioning."

The king continued, "The greatest men and women in my kingdom are quick to forget about what they accomplished many years ago. They seek me on a regular basis, and their confidence is in who I am and not what they have done. These humble ones have confidence in me based on what I have just taught them in the last seven days. Then, there are a very select few that wake up each morning with absolutely no confidence in their own abilities. As they ask me and rely only upon me, I impart to them everything they need for that day. I have called you to be one of those men."

This was a scary thought to me. Did I really want to forget *everything* I had done for the king?[32] Did I want the men to not trust me based on anything I had done in the past? I would certainly have to think about this for a while to make sure I wasn't just agreeing to this because I felt I was supposed to.

As I reflected on my past victories, I realized that any battle I had won was because I was relying on the king. With each successive victory, I became increasingly confident in my own ability to win. It was a very covert self-reliance. I was on the king's mission and winning the battles he planned for me to fight, which made it more difficult to discern that I was actually relying on my own strength.

"This city is not going to be changed by all your plans," he continued. "You will be better off throwing them all away."

This was a difficult thing to do since I had worked so zealously all day and felt that my basic intention to fix the town was good. I didn't mind a few slight modifications to the plans since I knew the king knew more than I did. However, I at least wanted to hang onto the papers with the plans so I could show my men how hard I worked. Even if I did throw them away, I at least wanted to figuratively hold on to them in my mental "back pocket" in case I needed to fix the town at some time in the future.

I was tempted to throw them in the garbage. I say "tempted" because this would allow me at least the opportunity to pull them out once the king had left and the men arrived. However, I had to trust the king fully. The fireplace needed some rekindling anyway.

I had thrown the plans in the fire but was still consoling myself, "At least my intentions were good!" As usual, the king knew exactly what I was thinking.

He responded to my internal justifications, "Many come here with good intentions, my son. They come to help, to fix, and to figure out, just as you came. Their planning is, just as yours was, based on their own experience. These people don't need an exportation of your culture to theirs. They certainly don't need to hear a proclamation of all the stereotypes against them. What they do need is an infusion of my kingdom *into* their culture."

12

ASIA

As I walked into a new town, I saw a group of what looked to be an Asian gang of boys in their late teens. The group appeared to be all high schoolers. They wore mostly black with some chains and various body piercings along with spiked hair. They were sitting on the side of the road and looked somewhat intimidating. I thought to myself, "I've never seen an Asian gang before." One of the boys who looked like the leader could read my thoughts, and he spoke out, "That's exactly what I'm talking about!" I didn't fully understand his response, and I was eager to talk with this group of teenagers, so I asked them all, "How's it going, guys?"

"What up, bro?" the leader responded with an urban accent. We began making small talk as I was not sure exactly what my mission was with these young men. They were clearly mature for their age and appeared more insightful than a typical street gang. The leader did not seem to be one who dominated the others, but, instead, he was more of a spokesman for the group. Thus, they felt free to speak with me but would occasionally look at the leader, wanting their words to line up with what he would say.

Seeing that I was still somewhat surprised by this gang, the leader spoke, "People expect us to sit around with books and calculators all day just because we're Asian. Then we go home, and our parents expect us to act and think just like them and the culture they were raised in. It's a no-win situation."

I could see this was a long-running battle that they had been waging in their minds for years. I've seen that youth join gangs because they are rejecting their personal weaknesses, their fathers, or their fear of those who push them around. These young men, however, were rebelling against who people expected them to be.

The gang leader continued, "Our parents think that unless we get perfect grades in school and band, we're disrespecting them. But, if we do what our parents want us to do, we're viewed as different at school. We're caught in the middle either way."

"And so you formed this gang," I concluded.

"Exactly," said the leader. "The funny thing is that most of us still live the life our parents want us to live. We don't wear these clothes around the house, and we somewhat comply with their expectations. Maybe they see that we're trying. I don't know. But we have an underlying frustration because we're not being who we really are, so that comes out in our behavior sometimes. They can't understand why we have an attitude toward them and their culture. There's definitely a disconnect at home."

As several of my other journeys previously taught me, there was no simple answer to this dilemma. I could understand that these young men felt caught in the middle between pleasing their parents and being socially accepted at school. It was a cultural gap that children from many countries have found themselves in. Even so, I wasn't totally excusing their behavior as they had clearly chosen to let their anger and rebellion set in.

As I spoke with the youth, my eyes were opened to the lives of the parents when their children were not around. This was a type of vision and insight that is not available in most kingdoms but is in this one. Given the disparity between the generations at home, I was surprised as I watched how the parents were speaking to other parents about their own children.

A number of the parents of the teenagers were sitting in a large high school auditorium concert hall, which probably seated over a thousand people. The seats were similar to those in a movie theater but more upscale. The stage had a black curtain with expensive looking red velvet around the edges. The large, black stage could comfortably fit a full choir but appeared to be set up for individual performances on this night.

As they waited for the musical performances to begin, the parents were talking about the accomplishments of their sons.

"My son just got an 'A' in math," a mother declared proudly.

"My son was star of the physics team," another whispered since the show was about to begin. I could see that the parents did not just behave like this at school events. They spoke of the accomplishments of their children whenever they were together. Each had one or two go-to statements about their children which they would declare to other parents. I could also see that, while all of them were very concerned about other aspects of their children's lives, they would only share accomplishments with other parents. Still, despite their talk of their children's feats, they often finished with comments like, "Well, *your* son is the better student," or "My son is not *nearly* as talented as yours." It was an intriguing game. They all seemed very familiar with the rules. On this night, the ones who were most proud were the parents of the most talented musicians. For all the dissension at home between the parents and their sons, at least for one hour, they could be proud of who their sons were in front of the other parents.

As the performances began, my consciousness left the concert hall and returned to the conversation with the youths in front of me. Although I had been watching what was happening in their parents' lives for a while, for the youths, it was as if I had just spoken to them a few seconds ago.

"Let me see what I can do," I told the leader and the other guys. He could see that I empathized with them and their predicament. Surprisingly, even though they just met me, they readily accepted me as a mediator between them and their parents. However, as I had realized many times before, things work differently in this kingdom than all other kingdoms.

As I journeyed to the other side of town to find the parents, I began to converse with the king, which was possible even though he was hundreds of miles away at the palace.

I asked him, "Why am I the one to solve this problem? Who am I to come in and fix all these issues that have been brewing for years?" I wasn't complaining when I asked him this. I simply did not want to be presumptuous to think that I was the "chosen one" to save this town.

The king explained, "It has to do with which missions I send you on and to whom I send you. There are many other peoples in my kingdom and many other towns to which I have not sent you. You are influencing these people and these towns because they are the ones I have sent you to influence. If you went to other towns, you would accomplish very little.[33] You would be frustrated and would either become self-critical or totally self-reliant and blame your lack of influence on the stubbornness of the people. But, as it stands, I have called you, I have prepared you, and I have equipped you."

I found that, as I grew older, the king's responses did not surprise me as much anymore. Through being with him in the palace and going on the missions on which he sent me, I had grown closer and closer to him. Walking with him became increasingly peaceful, and I understood his ways more. When he gave me a reply, it often captured what had been forming in my mind but could not yet fully formulate. I was not rebuked as often but was constantly being disciplined by him to fight more effectively. Yet, despite knowing him and his ways more, he was still in the habit of surprising me in ways that were special and personal.

I crossed to the other side of the town and entered a community center. To my amusement, hundreds of mothers and grandmothers were sitting in the bleachers of the gym and were waiting for me! As I stepped into the room, they immediately began with their cases against their boys.[34] While the boys had accepted me as their mediator after only knowing me for ten minutes, this assembly of Asian women accepted me as a mediator without ever having spoken to me!

"They don't respect us," one mother declared.

"They look down on us and our culture," two other mothers stated.

"They don't honor the authority of elders. They do whatever they feel like and always try to be exactly like the other teenagers around them," a mother called out, clearly representing the sentiment of many of the older ones in the room.

Though I knew this last statement was not completely the case, I could see where the mother was coming from.

Another woman further lamented, "We want them to get good grades in school and practice their instruments and excel beyond the other children. We want them to be excellent, and all they want to be is normal. We've sacrificed too much in coming to this country for them simply to be normal."

Many of the mothers and grandmothers made similar statements about grades and schooling and excelling in the school's band or orchestra. I noted that, although almost all their complaints revolved around school and performance, what really bothered them was that their boys did not respect them or their culture. In fact, the boys ran away from the culture as much as they could. I assumed that there were cultural implications I was facing that were beyond my grasp. I paused to take a moment to analyze the various complexities of the situation. I did not know how to proceed but was fully confident that the king's chief adviser Suelo would give me the right words to say.

"What is it you really want from them?" I asked the mothers.

The room quieted down for the first time since I had entered. The mothers knew I was not looking for them to give me another list of all the changes they wanted in their sons. They understood I was searching for the heart of the matter. Since I wasn't looking for a quick response, I gave them time to form a meaningful answer.

An older mother stepped forward and spoke in a quiet voice, "What we really want is for them to respect who *we are* and honor us as their parents and grandparents."

Most did not say anything after this. Some nodded their heads briefly. Everyone knew this mother had captured what they all truly desired. This was a turning point in reconciliation between the generations. However, I knew an additional step was needed.

"What do they truly want from you?" I asked them all.

Again, I waited for them to search their hearts. I could see it was very difficult for them to think like this. It was as if their thoughts were appearing above their heads like in a cartoon, and I could read every one of them. The mothers feared that if they acknowledged who their children had become, their children would take advantage of this and use it as a license to abandon their ancestors' culture. If they approved of their boys' new lifestyle, they feared their sons would never again respect them. This was what the mothers and grandmothers were trying to prevent all along.

I recalled how the king had once shared with me similar concerns he faced. He spoke to me about how easy it was for anyone to come into his palace and become his child. I had not thought about this at the time, but it made sense to me since all I had done was show up at his door every morning and walk with him around the palace. Eventually, one day, he invited me to live with him and be his son. The ease with which one became a child of the king was one of the things for which his enemies most ridiculed him. Even ones that lived in his palace but eventually rejected him and the palace leveled the same attacks against him. The accusation was that, since he made the path to his palace so effortless, his sons would take him for granted. Furthermore, since anyone off the streets was accepted, his sons would be just like the citizens of any other kingdom and would never attain to being great warriors or extraordinary people.

"What choice do I have?" the king had asked me. "I want all of those in the kingdom to come to my palace. It is true that there is only one entrance door to my palace, but it is not difficult to find for those who look for it. I will gladly endure the scoffs of the other kings and the other citizens. The road to sonship will always remain free."[35]

I was relieved to see that the mothers and grandmothers in the community center were ready to take the same risk the king had taken, to not fear their generosity being taken for granted. However, I could see one remaining roadblock facing a number of the women.

"Why do we have to be the ones to humble ourselves and take the first step?" some asked me, not out of bitterness, but mostly because this was uncharted cultural territory for them. They continued, "They are the ones that have rebelled against our authority. We're the leaders of the family. Shouldn't they be coming to us to apologize?"

I now was seeing why the king had trained me for so long before sending me on his missions. Since I had no children of my own at the time, I would have normally responded in a way that reflected my lack of experience in parenting. One who has been with the king has more wisdom than one with a hundred years of experience.

"You are right in saying that you're the leaders of the family," I answered. "And, as the leaders," I continued, "you must lead the way in humbling yourself so that your children may see you and follow your example. This is true leadership and is the true mark of authority."

I was about to declare, "This is an upside-down kingdom we live in," but stopped myself. They were all at least twice my age and did not need to hear all my thoughts on life. As I refrained from speaking words that would demonstrate my immaturity, an awareness of the king filled the community center. It was as if the king was anywhere and everywhere in that place. When the king comes, a change of heart always follows. The mothers and grandmothers now had a new mission. It was not to motivate their children to spend more time studying or to excel in a way that would bring acclaim to the family name. The mission was to restore their families.

I never did stick around to watch what happened that day. I could have watched. I'm sure it would have been heartwarming, but I felt like I wasn't supposed to stay around to see the outcome. I knew what would happen. The groundwork for the transformation of a village had been laid. After years of increasing division, the generations were finally headed toward reconciliation.

I'm not sure why the fruit of one's labor is not always immediately apparent. Maybe the king has so many people on his heart that he rushes sons away to help others before we see the end result. But it seems he knows our weaknesses and occasionally lets us see what our work has produced so that we are encouraged to continue loving more people.

I never talked again with any of the street gang or any of the mothers or grandmothers in the community center after that day. Around a year later, however, the king did allow me to briefly view the town. The transformation was astonishing. Mothers and sons walked the streets together, laughing, shopping, and enjoying each other. Teenagers were not embarrassed to be seen hanging out with their grandmothers. Sons listened to things important to their mothers and vice versa. I wasn't totally clear how these changes affected the students' academics, but I was pretty sure that, overall, the grades went down slightly. The mothers didn't seem to mind at all.

I saw many endearing sights as I watched that day, but one in particular has always stuck with me. I caught a glimpse of the gang leader walking with his grandmother on a sidewalk in front of a shopping promenade. The two were arm in arm, laughing, and seemingly more interested in spending time together than in finding whatever they were shopping for. To my surprise, the gang leader had not given up his all-black clothing, piercings, chains, and spiked hair. If anything, he had more piercings now. I had assumed he was just wearing those things to rebel against authority. Although many in the gang made different clothing choices after being united with their parents, the gang leader did not change his style because this was how he actually liked to dress! Even more fascinating, his grandmother had no trace of shame or embarrassment about her grandson's style. It was as if she was totally oblivious to how her grandson was dressed. Or, maybe, she was more aware than ever of how he dressed but didn't care one bit.[36]

13

WOMEN

As I ventured on, I soon found myself in a field with a multitude of women of all ages and backgrounds standing before me. In the kingdom, I usually walked to my destination, but, sometimes, I simply found myself in a new location without knowing how I got there. Now before me was an amazing sight to see. Thousands of women aligned in the shape of a large triangle with the woman at the front point directly facing me. The women all wore the same garments—iridescent, floor-length, white-and-gray-tinted robes. I had never considered gray a beautiful color, but these robes glowed as if they had a radiating life force flowing through them. It was as if purity—white—and wisdom—gray—emanated from each woman. I was filled with a healthy respect and honor as I beheld this massive gathering of the daughters of the king.

After standing in awe for a few moments, the woman in front approached me. "Michael,"[37] she said to me, her voice filled with both solemnity and honor that commanded my attention. I'm not sure why she called me by my middle name, but I sensed she had a pressing question on her heart, and I needed to hear it.

"Why is it that men pressure us to reveal our beauty to them, and, when we do, they either leave us or do not desire us anymore?"

I was quite surprised by this question not having previously thought along these lines with regards to male-female relationships.

Furthermore, I had expected that the woman would ask me about something related to the king. As I pondered her question, I surveyed the landscape of women before me, seeing into their hearts as only one in the kingdom is able. I saw that many of the women had extensive sexual pasts while some had no history of sexual activity. Many of the women related to the question posed to me. As if autobiographical movies floated above their heads, I saw that many of them had been pressured by men to give their bodies away prematurely.

Many of the single women had compromised their own sexual standards because men had coerced them. Subsequently, many of the men soon lost interest in the women and broke up with them to pursue other women who they believed were more desirable. Like the single women, numerous married women, while still married, experienced a similar detachment from their husbands. While still technically holding true to their marriage vows, the men's sexual desire for their wives had long ago waned. For years, the husbands had spent more time fascinated with female bodies in movies, on TV, and in magazines than with their own wives. This reality was clearly weighing heavily on the minds of the women. I knew that I needed to take action and was again amazed that I, the former orphan with no friends, was chosen to address an age-old dilemma.[38]

Then, I heard a young woman off to the side yell out, "Why do men never pursue us?" There was a quiver in her voice as she blurted out this question. I could tell from the other women that this young woman was not speaking on behalf of the others. A wise older woman looked at her lovingly and took her off to the side to comfort and counsel her. I was grateful for this older woman's help. I could have easily been derailed from the king's purpose for me in this place by devoting my energies toward extensive counseling sessions with this woman. What she needed was the mature wisdom of an older woman seasoned by experience.

I continued to gaze upon the crowd of women. I perceived that the king was the one who had given each woman her iridescent, white-gray robes to wear. These were among the greatest gifts the king could give. However, when they were around the men of the kingdom, the women often covered their robes. Because the women's apparel was so radiant, I assumed the women covered themselves for the sake of modesty.

"Why do the women do this?" I asked the woman in the front who had originally addressed me.

"We are grateful to the king for his robes for they are beautiful," she responded.

A taller, slightly older woman near the front continued, "But we do not always put them on around the men because we are not sure if they want us to wear them."

"They tell us they want our robes white," continued another woman, "but, from our experience, it seems they are often frustrated by the brightness of our robes. We know that the king has given us these robes to wear, but, around the men, we put on darker robes and multicolored robes. We're not blind. We see that many of the women with the most colorful robes receive the most attention from men. Sometimes, it is just easier to wear what the men like than what the king likes."

I cried out at the top of my lungs as I turned to the mass of men that now stood behind me opposite of the women, "Brothers, this should not be!"

The men had been listening in on the conversation. Many began to mumble excuses under their breath and became defensive. I overheard comments such as, "If she would just work out more!" or "I used to be attracted to her in white robes, but not anymore." Others were more philosophical, "I can't help it if I want an attractive wife," or "I'm wired this way; what do you expect?!" Some tried to turn things around on the women, saying, "She does the same thing to me!" It seemed as if they were not trying to convince anyone of their innocence. They were merely speaking without thinking as they were accustomed to doing when arguments arose at home with their wives.

Again, not knowing what I was going to say, I opened my mouth and explained, "The problem is not a matter of wanting a woman you are attracted to! The issue is that you are not attracted to the whiteness of their robes. Brothers, this should not be!"

As I was finishing confronting the men, I began to think, "Who am I to correct these men?" Memories of my own failures flashed before my mind such as flirting with the beautiful woman in the town of Ebony and behaving stubbornly in front of my men that day. Yet I once again felt the call of the king to speak forth and recalled his declaration to me that he would always use sons who were not yet perfected.

After waiting a while, I called out, "Men, LOOK!" and stepped out of the way, motioning for them to behold the sight of the vast array of women. I wish every man could see what the men and I beheld that day. I never use the word "beheld," but, that day, the men and I "beheld." We saw the women with totally new eyes. Before us was a mosaic of purity, honor, strength, and beauty. There were no words to describe the sight. The men and I simply stood in awe.

Definitively impacted and even transformed by one moment of true vision, the men began to speak among themselves concerning their wives. "I can't believe I didn't see her this way before!" "How could I have been unaware of who she really is?!" It was difficult for them to believe how great the disparity was between how they saw their women[39] in everyday life and how they beheld them now. A majestic sense of wonder pervaded the crowd. Soon, a concentrated yet peaceful determination arose in the men. Each husband was intent on pursuing reconciliation and winning back his wife's heart.

Suddenly, an awesome roar arose from the men. Men raised their fists, shouted at the top of their lungs, and charged directly toward the women. I felt as if I was right in the middle of an epic medieval battle. (Fortunately, I was not run over.) Amazingly, I looked over and saw the women were not frightened at all. In fact, they were pleased with this latest development and were completely at peace with the horde of men storming toward them.

Each man charged ahead, intent on finding his wife in the crowd. In their pursuit, they did not trample any of the women at the front.

Within a few minutes, each man found his wife in the crowd. As they held their wives, they spoke to them in a new way. I could not hear the individual conversations, nor did I need to. The unity, the reconciliation, and the oneness that took place spoke for itself.

Many men began to talk to the king about their women. The men would try to explain to the king saying, "King, I didn't realize..." or "King, I didn't see..." or "King, I had forgotten...." Each time, the king would answer them before they completed their sentence with, "I know." He was not interested in rebuking the men. Instead, his gaze was enough to tell them, "Continue to see them through this new lens of love."

After a while, the men began to bring the women over to the men's side of the field. To my surprise, the men did not do this because they were uncomfortable talking about their feelings. Nor were they uncomfortable being in the "women's section." Rather, each man took his wife to the men's side of the field in response to his wife's desire to go there. Also, surprisingly, the women didn't want to endlessly talk about their relationship with their husbands. Many of the men operated under the general notion that if women had their way, they would talk about "our relationship" and feelings all day, every day. It seemed that the women had pressured the men for these conversations only because many men had avoided such talk as much as possible.

The women did not want their relationships with their husbands to be the purpose of their lives. Furthermore, the women did not want to be the purpose of their husbands' lives. The women desired more in life and more from their marriage than just to talk about their relationship with their man. For the women, talking with the men about their relationship and their mutual love was not a destination but more of a refreshing rest stop along the journey. They had deep within them a desire to pursue the things important to the king. And they knew the desire of the men's hearts was to fight for the kingdom. The women were intent on finding where the kingdom destinies of the men intertwined with the kingdom destinies of the women.

It is amazing how the men's change of perspective transformed their behavior. This behavior change in the men then led to an equally powerful metamorphosis in the way the women responded to the men. As a result, the perennial stalemate in the battle of the sexes took a step forward that day.

14

VANITY MIRRORS

Sometime later, I was back in the palace with the king. He took my hand and led me to a corridor that I had never seen before. It continually amazed me that for as long as I had been here, I never exhausted experiencing new areas of the palace nor the truths that were obtained in each room. We stepped into a long hallway lined on both sides with sinks and accompanying vanity mirrors. Each identical mirror was framed with gold and had a bright light above it. I never counted them, but the hallway must have contained at least sixty mirrors on each side.

Intrigued by the sight, I turned to the first mirror on my right to check my appearance. I figured that if I was to pass by so many mirrors in a well-lit room, I should at least make sure I looked decent. I fixed my hair quickly and made sure I didn't have anything sticking to my face.

I turned to walk down the corridor and thought, "Since there's a second mirror here, I might as well check my appearance one more time just to be safe."

I took another step down the hallway and decided to utilize the third mirror. I had only checked my face and hair before, so I thought it would be worth it to ensure my clothes matched and were not too wrinkled. The clothes I wore looked good and so did my hair. Seeing my appearance was satisfactory, I had more confidence to walk down the hallway with the king.

"So, why are there so many mirrors in this hallway?" I asked the king. He drew me with his hand to step backwards and directed my attention toward a young woman at the entrance of the hallway. He had just finished a brief conversation with her.

I watched the woman stop at the first mirror on the right just as I had done. She spent a lot of time there, putting on eyeliner, curling her eyelashes, and putting on makeup. Ten or fifteen minutes must have passed before she deemed herself ready to proceed. She turned to walk down the hallway but immediately stopped to check her appearance in the second vanity mirror. I was surprised to see her spend at least as much time at the second mirror despite having spent significant time fixing herself up just seconds ago.

Again and again she turned, utilizing the third mirror and the fourth and the fifth and the sixth and so on. Each time she found something new on her face to which to attend. After being unsatisfied with her brown hair after appearing before several mirrors, she dyed her hair blonde. Soon, her preference for her blonde color quickly waned, and black became the next color of choice. Interestingly enough, she actually thought she would look worse with black hair, but, since it was time to change her hair color, she decided she needed to do this.

In a manner only possible in the kingdom, I watched several years of this woman's life transpire before us. Day after day and in mirror after mirror, the woman would stop to fix her appearance. She repeated this ritual incessantly. Since each mirror demanded ten or fifteen minutes, this aspect of her life took a considerable amount of time.

I did not pay attention to each time she stopped, since it was the same basic routine over and over again. I noticed that when she had made it to the end of the hallway, she looked beautiful. However, she had looked beautiful to me when she first entered the hallway without the hours, even years, of adjustments in front of the vanity mirrors. The king then had me look at her reflection in the mirrors rather than at the woman directly. To my amazement, in each mirror along the way, her face grew increasingly unattractive. By the last mirror, her countenance had turned brown and green with warts and pus coming out of her face. It was truly difficult to watch.[40]

"Why does she still look beautiful when I look at her at the end of the hallway, but, when I look at her in the mirror, her face is so distorted?" Not waiting for an answer, I continued, "Which one is how she really is? How I see her, or how she appears in the mirror?"

The king explained, "The mirror and the light from the mirror show all and reveal all. What you see in the mirror is what she is, that is, what she has become. Yet, even so, the light reveals not who she really is, but who she has made herself to be."

I was deeply impacted by this sight and by the condition of this woman. I felt compassion for her, knowing that she had labored in vain year after year only to achieve the opposite results of what she was hoping for. I wondered what she was thinking, and, more importantly, if there was anything that could save her from this vicious cycle she was in.

I thought back to when she first entered the hallway. She looked beautiful both in person and in the mirror. I assumed this was normal since I didn't know at the time that people could look so differently in their reflection. I reasoned that since she looked beautiful in both views and because she had come from the palace, that she was a daughter of the king. After all, I too had stopped to look several times in the vanity mirrors before feeling comfortable or secure enough to continue walking with the king. Looking back on it now, I wasn't concerned about looking good for the king. I was thinking about looking good for others if they happened to come into the hallway. When I first came to the palace and didn't know the king, I always tried to look my best and be on my best behavior. But, after knowing him for so long, I usually didn't concern myself with trying to give him the best impression of me. Unfortunately, this often led me to take him for granted. "He'll accept me however I am," I reasoned. It was true, but this had too often become a license to blow him off.

Slowly, my thoughts drifted back to the woman at the end of the hallway. I still had a lot of questions in my mind because I was still taken aback by what had occurred in this woman's life. As usual, the king knew each question racing through my mind. He used to answer my questions without me asking, but, as I matured, he often waited until I asked him. After several years of friendship with him, I had learned to not just blurt out questions but to ask him the questions for which I really wanted answers. Much of the time, I did not even have to ask the king to understand things. Often, I simply had to search the motives of my heart, using the insight he had already given me, and the issue became clear. When searching my heart met its limit, I would then ask the king.[41] In this way, I grew in wisdom and understanding, and, in the process, grew as a man.

I was going to ask him why I had felt the need to stop by the first few mirrors, but realized I already knew the answer. I still had elements of vanity in my own life: spending too much time in front of the mirror, expecting people to treat me better if I was dressed nicely, and taking pride in my hair, even though I did not have as much anymore! However, this same pride in my appearance quickly turned to shame if I had old clothes on or if something in my appearance was out of place. As much as I was incredulous over the woman's actions, I had the same inclinations in my own heart. I was just better at hiding it.

After reflecting on my own shortcomings, I asked the king, "Why is the hallway connected to the palace?" This was something I truly did not understand. "It seems to only have a negative effect on people!"

The king responded, "I will make many to pass through this hallway. It is true that many of my children are caught in this hallway and some never escape. But those who pass through and are not ensnared by the mirrors have a focus like few have. They do not lust after the attention they can get from people or the temporary accolades they can garner for themselves. They see human praise for what it is, fickle and fleeting. These overcomers are not distracted by what's on the left or the right. Their focus is on what is ahead, and they know the foolishness of investing in outward appearance. Truly, many will be made to pass through this hallway in the coming days."

This was the first time I had heard the king talk about the future. Yet, all along, there had been a growing awareness in me that a great climax, a consummation of all that transpired in the kingdom, was coming. While my brothers and I had trained and worked for years to bring others to the palace, a day was coming when those in the kingdom would no longer have the option whether or not to follow the king. Some would come to the palace because it was the lifelong desire of their heart; others would come by force. The king's throne of intimacy would one day become a throne of judgment. I had seen glimpses of this for years,[42] and, as the years passed, the reality of this future culmination became more and more clear. This grand finale amazed me, bewildered me, and even terrified me. Yet, even so, I longed for it to come.

Again, my attention came back to the hallway. By this time, another woman had entered the hallway and begun working on her appearance in front of the first mirror. She continued on the same path as the first woman, and, likewise, her appearance grew worse the farther along the hallway she progressed. While the process was the same for both women, I noticed their attitudes were markedly different. I couldn't quite put into words the difference.

"How do *they* see themselves at the end of the hallway?" I asked the king.

He responded with a question, "They both look beautiful when you look at them, do they not?"

"They do," I agreed.

"And they both look unattractive when you look at them in the vanity mirror, do they not?"

"They do," I again concurred.

"They both look beautiful on the outside yet are rotting away on the inside. Still, the second woman in her own mind grows more and more beautiful with each mirror she arrives at. As she grows increasingly impressed with her appearance, she becomes increasingly critical of the appearance of women around her.

"The first woman only sees what we see in the mirror, the filth and decay. Unfortunately," he continued, clearly grieved for her, "she considers the blemishes to only be on the outside. She is almost completely blind to the impact her obsession is having on the inside. She is less and less aware of those around her. To be honest, she doesn't even care very much about herself anymore, just her image."

"Which state are more women caught in?" I asked.

"Most are drawn to the downfall of the first woman in the hallway. With each passing year, they construct new ways to 'fix' their appearance. Their struggle grows deeper each year. More makeup can't fix the problem. Magazines can't fix this disease. Their friends can't either. Not even marriage, as some would think, can cure them."

"Then what can we do for them?" I asked, exasperated by the situation and desperate to do something for my sisters following this path.

"You will go talk to her," the king said, referring to the first woman who was still standing ashamed of herself in front of a mirror at the end of the hallway. He knew I had no idea what to say to the woman, but, as he sent me, he smiled mischievously at me as if to say, "I will continue to send you as my answer to the problems you see."

I hadn't seen this directive coming. I was at a loss as to how I could possibly help this woman break free from this vicious cycle. However, like other assignments from the king, I knew that if I held to what he taught me, I would have the right words at the right time. Also, as I had learned from the town of Ebony, it was more important to love people than to try to fix them. Though not knowing what to say as I approached the woman doing her makeup in the mirror, I felt nothing but love for this woman.

"Can I help you?" I asked, feeling dumb for asking this. It's definitely not normal to randomly walk up to someone and ask her how you can help. This was not one of those times when the words of my mouth felt as if they were directly from the king.

"No," she replied matter-of-factly without looking up. "I'm just fixing up a few things."

I didn't know how to respond, but I was suddenly frustrated with her. I felt like yelling, "You just 'fixed up' sixty times!"

I had to quickly let my frustration go. This was about her, not me. "Why do you need to fix up?" I asked.

"To look good for the world, you know?"

"I can't say I do," I said sincerely. "Why do you need to look good for the world?"

Now it was her turn to be frustrated with me. "You males are the reason I have to put myself through all this!"

"You don't have to do this for me," I protested.

"Maybe not you, but for almost every other guy out there, I do. And so I do it day after day after day!"

She felt the need to defend herself but didn't want to argue with me. I could see she wasn't mad at me but was worn out by years and years of playing this same game. Neither of us knew what to say, so we just stood there somewhat unsure of how to proceed. She wasn't used to speaking honestly about this topic, especially with a guy that actually cared about her.

"What's your name?" I asked her.

"Lisa," she responded.[43]

"Lisa," I said, this time with compassion instead of frustration, "you don't have to spend all this time making yourself look better."

She seemed ready to open up to me. "Every time I date a guy, he thinks I'm beautiful in the beginning. I begin to trust him, and I bare my heart to him. Then, for some stupid reason, it hits a point where he suddenly doesn't want me anymore. Before, he couldn't stop thinking about me, but, now, I annoy him. I never know if it's something I did or if he is just a bad guy, but it happens with guy after guy. They can't *all* be bad..." she said, her voice trailing off and her eyes gazing into the distance. "So I do what I can to find the best clothes, the best makeup, and the best jewelry. Yet, some other girl always wins..." she said, trailing off again.

At this, she stared at the floor, ashamed of herself as memories streamed through her mind. After a while, she muttered, "So what am I supposed to do?"

The "What am I supposed to do?" question played in my mind for a while. I really wanted to give the right answer. "Oh, king," I thought, "help me say something to help this precious woman."

"You can go talk to the king," I suggested, knowing this was the right answer but feeling like this was too simplistic of a solution.

"I tried before. It didn't work."

"I know you did; I saw you."

"What do you mean you saw me?"

"I saw you right after you talked with the king." She didn't understand what I was saying but wasn't looking to argue with me.

"You tried talking with the king," I continued, "but he wasn't looking for a one-time conversation. He wants you to know him and be free to be yourself with him. When this happens, you start to see yourself as he sees you."

I paused to give her a moment to think about this and also because I felt foolish. I felt like this was the tritest advice I had ever given. I was accustomed to being surprised by the great wisdom that proceeded from my mouth in situations like this. But, now, I assumed this woman and every other woman had heard a million times before a pat answer like "Just go to the king. He'll make everything better." I had been hoping for and expecting some great revelation, knowing that the king had sent me to talk to her. Nothing came to me, but I had to say something. So, I just continued to speak in very generic and seemingly lifeless terms.

After we spoke for a little while longer, she accepted my offer to come back to the king. With a brief smile, she turned to walk down the long corridor with me. As soon as she smiled, I had this sudden desire to impress her. It felt good to have a beautiful woman trust me and smile at me. Several ways to get her to be impressed with me or think that I was funny popped into my mind. Maybe I could be the guy to finally make her feel good about herself.

In hindsight, it's ironic that just moments after declaring the king as the answer to her greatest need I was immediately inclined to become the answer to a void in her that I could never personally fill. Maybe there was some emptiness in me which I was looking to her to fill. Either way, this was obviously not what the king had in mind when he sent me to be the answer to the problem I saw.

We approached the king, who had been at the entrance of the doorway watching our entire interaction.

"What can I do for you?" he asked, looking at me.

"My friend wants to see how you see," I said on her behalf.

"Is this true?" he asked her. It seemed important for him to hear it directly from her.

"Yes," she answered, quietly, yet confident that this was what she wanted. Though I had just met her, I was so proud of Lisa for the courage I saw in her.

"Come. Take a walk with me," he said, taking her arm in his. As he turned away, he motioned to me with a nod that he would take care of her from here.

I watched as the two went up to the king's balcony. There was no greater view in the kingdom than from the king's balcony. The two sat gazing at a magnificent purple mountain range in the distance with the sun setting just above it.

"Do you see the beauty of these mountains?"

"I do," Lisa answered.

"And the beauty of the sun?" he continued.

I realized this was a personal conversation, and, although I had the ability in the kingdom to view this conversation from afar, it was best that I did not. I'm not aware of everything the king said to Lisa that day, but I knew he compared her beauty to that of the mountains and the sun. For the first time, she believed a man's affirmation of her value.

This sight plays in my mind often. I wish many women could hear what Lisa heard from the king that day. I believe many have heard it but not many have *really* heard it. That day changed her forever. All of her repetition, all of her dedication, and all of her striving in the Hall of Vanity Mirrors was broken off of her that day. The reality of her beauty in the sight of the king forever liberated her.

I saw the king later that night after he finished talking with Lisa. I was grateful to see my sister set free but was still a little upset that I didn't have anything more profound to say to her.

"What happened back there?" I asked him. "I felt like anyone could have expressed what I said to her! I would think that after being with you for years, I could have come up with something better than that. A child could have told her, 'Go to the king.'"

"That's the point," the king responded. "I sent you to Lisa to bring her to me. You wanted to bring her to yourself, which is why you tried to impress her. And you wanted to say something profound that would make an impact on her so that you could feel good about yourself. But I wanted to set her free and show her what *I* could do for her."

I felt ashamed when I heard this. It was not a shame where I was condemning myself. Rather, this was the shame I had learned to love because I knew that I always grew from these moments. The king rebuked me as a child because he was making me a man.

"I wanted to represent you well," I said, not disagreeing with him but wanting to express my heart to him. "You're so full of wisdom. Every time you speak, it impacts people's lives. There's such power behind your words. I just wanted to be like you."

While I had been focusing this whole time on the void in Lisa's life, I was suddenly acutely aware of my need for wholeness. As I became aware of my own lack of wisdom, insight, pure motives, and a host of other things, I was filled with a longing to be more like the king. This was not so that I could get people to think I was wise but because his thoughts and his words superseded all others. Everything he said was full of peace and life. It was as if my entire being was at rest when I listened to him and understood him. I didn't have any time for self-pity when I was with him.

This was the first time I understood that, though I was becoming a man, I would always be a child to him. I had always had the sense that I would have to grow up to the point that I didn't have anything childlike in me. It seemed that being a child was a negative thing, something to run from if I really wanted to be mature. I had been made to feel ashamed for being childish by many while I was growing up. The insinuations of being immature had taken a toll on me over the years. I had lived my life under the continual cloud of the impossible standard that I "needed to be a man."

"You will always be my son," the king affirmed at a moment when I needed to hear it from him.

"When you go to battle with me, you go out as my son. When you train with me, you train as my son. When you fight for me and with me and because of me, you fight as my son. In everything, you will always be a child. And you will always be my son."

His message sunk in. I had always enjoyed being his son but never thought of our father-son relationship when on the battlefield. Moreover, my thoughts of training, fighting, and achieving victories on the battlefield seemed completely incompatible with being a child. Yet, for the first time in my life, I didn't flee from the thought of always being a child.

Once again, the king was teaching me a new way to fight.

15

THE LAST BATTLE

"**I**t is more important for you to fearlessly trust me than for you to know all the details," the king told me.

After hearing these words, we suddenly appeared at a battlefield where several groups of the king's sons were preparing for battle. Our troop was to form in lines four or five men deep and could not have totaled more than 300. I looked past our armies across a field and saw that we were far outnumbered by the enemy's forces. Several thousand of the enemy's troops were advancing in a semicircle formation with the top of its arc being farthest from us. My immediate inclination was to take control of the situation. I had gained much wisdom in battle and was not about to let my brothers be destroyed. If they were going to pull off this victory, they needed the strategy of a lifetime.

However, before I could develop my own plan, the king informed us of his strategy. The troops were to approach the battlefield and fight the enemy as they approached. I waited for more information, but that was the only instruction he gave. It sounded like a gross oversimplification of what was necessary for victory, and it also seemed highly irresponsible to not provide further details.

"Are you serious?" I yelled in my mind. I continued, "Maybe if we had them outnumbered two to one this would work but not when they are ten times the size of our army!"

I had to do something. I couldn't let my brothers go into battle with an inferior strategy and watch them get demolished.

"The king's always right," played in my mind. I knew that, but I was tired of that answer.

"Maybe he's gotten too old," I pondered. "Maybe he's using plans that worked in the past but are no longer effective. I don't know what he's thinking, but he's going to get everyone killed."

I began to consider gathering the leaders of the troops to employ another plan. Since the enemy was approaching in a semicircle formation, I knew that they would soon surround our small line of troops. We would have to either retreat or find a way to come around behind them. Either way, a head-on conflict was certain to be disastrous.

However, before I could organize the other leaders to implement a plan, the troops were sent out to fight. I saw groups comprised of ten of the king's soldiers camp out on little hills by trees and bushes. The enemy, on the other hand, would only send out three or four troops at a time despite possessing a massive army. As these small groups of enemy troops would approach the hills, the king's troops easily picked them off one by one. Repeatedly, the enemy sent his troops in threes and fours to attack the king's formation, yet the king's army kept easily picking off the approaching soldiers. This went on for a long time until the enemy had suffered many casualties. After several hours of this, the enemy called off the battle and retreated away from the battlefield.

I was astonished at how easily we won the battle, yet I couldn't bask in the glory of the victory. I knew I had been wrong. The king knew I had planned to gather troops to counter his strategy. I had learned to love the king's rebukes because I knew I always matured as a result of them. However, this time, I hadn't just defied him, I had also intended to recruit others to disregard his orders. This time, I was sincerely ashamed to approach the king.

The king had a stern but calm look on his face as I approached him. We both knew that I had committed a more serious offense this time, yet he did not rebuke me.

"What happened out there?" I asked the king. "How did you know?"

"Because I've seen him do this over and over," he responded.

"But the enemy's not stupid. Why would he use such a poor strategy?"

"He's usually more concerned with bragging about the size of his army and showing off to his friends than he is about winning. He knew his army was far bigger than mine. That's one of his constant accusations against me: More people would rather follow him than me."

"He probably knew he was going to incur heavy losses in this battle, but he's not really concerned about the lives of his troops. He is always recruiting. For him, losses are often wins."

"When he brags about the size of his army, how do you respond?" I asked curiously

"I don't respond to him. I don't need to," he answered.

"But doesn't it look bad if people only hear his side of the story? Doesn't it make *you* look bad?"

"For many, his side of the story is enough. He lets his recruits do whatever they want. But, for those who really want to, they always find me. And, if they don't, I search for them, and I always find them."

As I listened to the king describe the enemy's tactics and brazen disregard for the life of his troops, the enemy's wickedness seemed palpable. I had always viewed the enemy as a nebulous force to avoid on the other side of the mountain. He was nameless and faceless. I assumed that he didn't have plans or agendas, but I was beginning to see that he was purposeful and strategic. I saw that he was a general, or, to better describe how he operated, a militant dictator. Just as the king extended a personal, customized invitation to each person in the kingdom, the enemy devised tailored invitations for people. However, unlike the king, he enticed people based on their unique weaknesses and vulnerabilities. The soldiers in his army were actually somewhat effective fighters, and I assumed the king would show me more about the enemy's soldiers later.

I drifted back to thinking about our approach to the enemy in this last battle. I was still curious as to why we did not send all of our troops onto the battlefield. It seemed to me that even though we won the battle we could have won even more decidedly. The king began to replay the battle before my eyes. I saw beyond where our troops had confronted the enemy's troops. As I looked past the field and into the enemy camp, I noticed more of the king's men plundering the enemy almost unhindered. Of course, at the time, I hadn't seen this was taking place. I had thought either the king was being foolish or he was just trying to give us some kind of test to teach us a lesson. I didn't even know the king had more armies at his disposal.

"Because I only sent a few contingents into this battle, others were freed up to fight elsewhere," the king explained.

I had always thought the best strategy was to send as many as possible to fight. It always bothered me that no matter where I went in the kingdom, more opposed the king than stood in favor of the king. I usually thought to myself, "If we just had a few more of my brothers here, then we would have the victory." That day, I saw that it was not the number of troops in the battle that was most important. The key to victory was following the king's strategy.

I continued thinking about the size of the king's army. I realized that I had slowly developed a mindset that people did not really want to know the king. It was funny that I would think that way since I had experienced such joy, contentment, and freedom in my interactions with the king. Moreover, I had witnessed many others go through the same process. Frequently, I had the joy of watching others exclaim, "I can't believe how good this is!" as they encountered the king and the palace for the first time.

Yet, those who turned away seemed more etched in my mind than those who remained with the king. It so broke my heart to see even one abandon the king in order to return to their former life. I had almost grown into the mindset of, "I don't want people to leave the palace, so I'm not going to tell them about it in the first place." Of course, I didn't actually say this, but the way I had lived my life revealed my mindset.

I knew the king's thoughts towards those who left. He loved them. He always had a special place in his heart for those who had come to the palace for a time. Knowing this, I was still concerned about my attitude. The king had become a burden to me at times. More precisely, the king was a burden to some of those who I had invited to the palace, and thus, I made their burden mine. It's a terrible feeling to realize the greatest love of your life has become a burden to you.

"Why would I think this way?" I asked myself. Some of the responses of people over the years appeared in my mind. Some said it seemed that the notion of a palace, a loving king, unlimited feasting, and the best military training in the world all in one place was too good to be true. I knew the young professionals initially had this impression until they were branded with the fire that poured into their hearts. Fortunately, these men had accepted the invitation of the king.

When I saw instant transformations like this, it was so fun and easy to tell people about the king afterward. But after a string of people called me an idiot or told me I was crazy and old-fashioned, my excitement would wane. I had heard it all. "You're dreaming, buddy!" "I don't need an adopted father. I already like the dad I have!" Some were harsher and more condescending: "Oooh, we're going to fly away to a magical castle in a faraway land!" Of course, laughing at me would soon ensue. In these moments, I was still able to remember the most glorious times I had had with the king. These times just did not seem very glorious amid this mocking that had taken a toll on me. I knew that I had let others steal my joy.

"What's happened to me?" I asked the king. I'm sure if I thought about it a while, I could have formulated a number of reasons why I had become hesitant and fearful. By now, though, many times I would ask a question even if I already thought I knew the answer because I would always get more insight. Sometimes, I just needed to hear the answer from the king's mouth. I would have the exact thought in my head, yet, when he spoke it, his words were life to me. Many in the greatest seats of the Halls of Wisdom were there not because they had all the answers but because they spent their lives asking the right questions.

"Because," the king answered my previous question, "you care more what they *think* than what you *know*."

This was pretty much the answer I was expecting.

"But, ultimately, you're thinking more about yourself than about them. You're the one who has experienced the palace; they haven't."

I already knew I had only been thinking about myself and my reputation in these situations, but I needed to hear it from him. I loved the times of new understanding, but I probably had more need for the times when he reiterated what he had already taught me. When we had one of these types of conversations, it was as if I re-realized in a fresh way what I had already realized.

One might think that after listening to the king for years, the amazement at his wisdom would wear off. It never did. I lived a life perpetually in awe of my adopted father.

The Parade

After the battle was finished, I found myself sitting on a balcony near the top of a building. Down below vast crowds of people lined both sides of a barricaded street. The king's sons, clothed in battle garb, paraded triumphantly through the town as the king, dancing through the streets, led the procession.[44] The jubilant crowds cheered them on by waving flags, chanting victory songs, and congratulating the passing soldiers. These people had celebrated victories before, but this was unlike any celebration the kingdom had ever known. This victory was final. Never again would there be another battle. It was truly a joyous occasion for the people.

However, I was very confused by this event. The king came and joined me to watch.

"Father, how can this be the final victory celebration? What about the great last battle? I've felt in my heart for years that it was coming one day!"

"Many battles have been fought,[45] and many were more intense than the one you fought. For years I have sent your brothers all over the kingdom on their own missions. You thought that your mission was the greatest and you were the only one who I was sending on a great mission. This was because it was so personal to you. For you, your mission was the greatest mission. Yes, all the battles have already been fought.[46] And not only have they been fought, they have been won."[47]

I later watched the same euphoric crowds again lining the same street below me, cheering as the defeated army was marched before our eyes. I knew that they were being paraded one last time before their destruction. It surprised me that the crowd cheered in a similar fashion at the sight of the enemy army marching in a parade of defeat as they had in support of our soldiers marching in victory. I knew these enemy soldiers had fought against the king and had sought to destroy his sons, yet it seemed cruel to rejoice in their defeat.[48] I knew the king wanted each person in that procession to be his son. He had reached out to their regions of the kingdom over and over again. He had endless methods of reaching out to people and continually created new ways of inviting people to the palace. I understood all of this, and my heart broke as I considered the fate of the defeated ones. I knew each one was awaiting punishment.

As I watched with conflicting emotions of celebration and heartbreak, the king came up to the balcony and joined me.

About to cry, I asked, "Are you happy, King?"

"I am."

"How can you be happy at a time like this?"

"I am happy because my sons and I have conquered, and we have finally won the battle."

"But what about all the defeated ones being led to the slaughter? I know you love each one! How can you rejoice when they are all about to be destroyed?"

"I weep for them."

"Then why don't you do something about it? Can you really rejoice and weep at the same time?"

"I can."

"That doesn't make any sense!"

"If there is a good judge in the land," he said turning to me to explain, "the people are secure and they rejoice. Now, imagine that the judge's own son has trespassed the law and has robbed and destroyed a family. When his son comes before him in court, will he not have him punished under the due process of the law of the land? And, though difficult for him, he will have peace at night knowing that justice has not been perverted but preserved. Not only will he rejoice, but the whole land will also rejoice with him over the justice that prevailed. They will say, 'Surely if he will be fair and bring justice even to his own son, he will bring justice for all. How he treats his son, he will surely treat us.'"

The king continued, "Now, suppose that he sentences his son to twenty-seven years in prison. If the son changes his ways and honors the guards and is good to the other prisoners, will not the father, as a good judge, take notice? Will he treat his son the same as the man in the next cell who has attacked his fellow prisoners and disobeyed and berated the prison guards? Of course not. He will have compassion on his son, and, at the allotted time as established by the courts, he will release his son early for good behavior[49] and his change of heart. Thus, the judge will be both just and full of compassion. And, again, all the land will hear of it and take note."

He then looked me in the eyes and with great seriousness and love, said, "So, I too rejoice in justice and delight in compassion."

16

THE FINAL PALACE CALL

After the great and glorious battle, I joined the king on the day the troops returned from the parade. I saw the king seated on his throne. It appeared to be the same throne where I had first sat with him, but the setting had changed. The king was seated in the middle of a room, and on each side behind his throne were large doors. All of the inhabitants of the kingdom were before the throne. Two lines formed, one on each side of the king. Among them were the greatest sons of the kingdom, those who hated the king, those who didn't believe the king existed, and various others with varying viewpoints about the king. The sons of the king formed a massive line leading up to the right side of the king's throne, and those who opposed the king formed a massive line leading up to the left side of the king. It was quite a sight to see people who for decades denied that the king existed now standing before him.

The scene before me was terrible, awe-inspiring, and glorious all at the same time. I had seen this consummation of all things in front of the king for many years.[50] This was the time when all, great and small, young and old, would once and for all gather before the king. Yet, for years, I had only seen merely a glimpse of this final scenario. What I knew would one day unfold was now upon me.

I could not see far beyond the two doorways at the end of each procession. However, what lay beyond them was clear to all. Behind the doorway on the king's right was a feast unlike anything we had ever taken part of. No fellowship table in the palace could ever compare to this jubilant banquet. There was only an unrivaled joy, celebration, and unity of purpose. In this new realm, there were no training grounds, no garden, and no missions to be sent on, only continuous feasting and elation. The pictures in the Hall of Fame had been taken down. The men and women in the Hall were no longer just memories. They were alive and joined together with all the heroes who had ever lived. All were united in joyful celebration forever.

I could see very little beyond the great doorway on the left side of the king. I didn't need to see even if I could. Everyone on both sides of the line knew what lay behind that door. Misery unlike anything ever known in the kingdom awaited the multitudes. Some had already gone through the door; they were already languishing in agony, crying out for relief. Yet we knew all too well that there was no end to the torment ahead.

Having seen this one sight for years, I knew it would come. I never wanted to think about it but simply could not keep my mind from visualizing this final scenario. Its reality would flash before my eyes in the midst of an intense battle or in the midst of a long talk with the king. Yes, I knew it would come. I just never wanted to dwell on it.

Now was the final time to ask the king about these things. Even though he was sitting on his throne of judgment, I could speak with him face to face as a friend. He was like no other king. I had to ask him the questions that nagged at my mind and had burdened my heart for years. I couldn't hold the burning questions inside any longer.

"How could you let people go there, Father?" I cried out in despair. "I know you're loving! I know you love those people! If I love them, and I do, I know you love them ten times more! I know they've done wrong. I know they've rejected you. They've rejected me. They've rejected my brothers time and time again! But why such severity? Why does it have to be so tormenting? Why does it have to be forever? Father, how could you do this!?" With this last line, I fell down before him, weeping at his feet. I held nothing back and sobbed uncontrollably before the throne. I had never poured out my heart like this before. My only hope was that the king would finally give me an answer. I knew he would.

The king responded, "I have done this because I am jealous for you." His words pierced my heart like a sword. I was so moved partly because his response caught me totally off guard and partly because I felt like this was the first time I began to comprehend this reality. Still, I didn't fully grasp what he was saying.

The king elaborated, "I am eternally jealous for you. If I let others into where you are going, I would never have you. They would continually defile you. They would continually hate you. They would continually sling mud at you and curse you and do everything in their power to keep you from me. There would be no rest, no peace, and no joy in the place you are going if there was nothing behind that doorway on my left."

"I could give them more time in the kingdom," he continued, directly responding to the question that was raging in my mind. "I've tried that. They only grew to hate me more and more.[51] And not only me, but they increasingly despise my children. It is to their advantage that I have limited their time in the kingdom. Otherwise, their torment would be far worse."[52]

He then turned to me with deep compassion in his eyes and said, "Yes, my beloved son, it is because of my love for you that you are in the place of complete joy on the right and they are in the place of consuming agony on the left. For it is in casting them out that I bring you in."[53]

ENDNOTES

Chapter 1
The Journey Begins

1 **The shock of being asked to be the king's son:** Although this was a vision and I was raised by my biological parents in real life, I believe I felt the full weight of the surprise and joy an orphan would feel after finally belonging to someone.

Chapter 2
Entering the Palace

2 **Battles hinging on a single weapon:** This room and the message of this room contained overtones of some of the epic battles of the Book of Judges as well as King David's battles. The focus was not the weapons or artifacts themselves but rather obedience to the uniquely prescribed pathway to victory.

3 **The throne room was empty except for the king:** In heaven, the throne room of God is obviously not empty (Revelation 4:4; Revelation 14:3). Despite constant interaction with countless humans and spiritual beings, God is still the God of one-on-one, personal intimacy.

4 **Pure joy of dancing:** Even as I was watching this vision, the joy and deep contentment I felt was overwhelming. To this day, that experience was one of the most satisfying of my life.

5 **All you have to do to be great is to walk with me:** I believe greatness is one of the most misunderstood concepts among Christians. Despite Jesus repeatedly emphasizing that the child and the least among us

are the greatest, people still miss the point. Too often, crowd size, book sales, and social media followers are viewed as indicators of greatness. Here, relationship is presented as the key to greatness.

6 **Distracted by ghost-boys:** Not being distracted or intimidated by what outsiders may think is still one of the primary challenges I face daily.

7 **Ghost-boys throughout the entire kingdom:** After the Last Day, there will be no more ghost-boys/mockers. Until then, wherever the king and his children go mockers will follow.

Chapter 3
Training Grounds

8 **Exaltation of heroes of the past:** The glorification and borderline idolatry of past heroes has kept many from seeing the most important battles of today. We are called to honor spiritual ancestors, not idolize them. Pharisees of Jesus' day decorated tombs of the prophets, but Jesus said they would have murdered the prophets had they been alive (Matthew 23: 29-32). Likewise, many today pay homage to saints of old but would persecute these righteous ones if they were alive today.

9 **Never fight a battle they can't win:** From the outside, it may appear that many of our battles are lost. Yet, supposed failures and successes are not always as they seem. Disgrace, insults, and even death are often not failures but victories. Every battle we are called to fight possesses potential for growth and maturity, which are victories in and of themselves.

10 **Adviser Suelo:** I intuitively understood that Suelo was part of the Triune Godhead. Just as Jesus never told a parable that detailed the exact nature of the Trinity, so too the Lord did not provide me with a comprehensive explanation of the Trinity in these visions.

11 **Those who could excel in one area:** The world has many "Samsons" who are impressive in one area but morally deficient in others. More who have been formed and molded in many areas like Daniel are needed. Excellence as a theologian, preacher, or teacher is significantly mitigated if other areas of one's life are mired in immaturity and compromise.

12 **Life requires one great revelation after another:** Every truth and every principle in life has already been revealed through Jesus Christ and through God's Word, the Bible. However, no one instantly understands and fully lives out all of these truths. We need ever-increasing revelation and insight into what has already been revealed. Similarly, King David possessed God's Word in the form of the Torah, the collection of Moses' writings which comprise the first five books of the Bible. Though David intellectually knew God's law through these writings, he prayed to the Lord, "Open my eyes that I may see wonderful things in your law" (Psalms 119:18).

Chapter 4
The Garden

13 **Having me labor on my own:** Clearly, God never leaves his children (Psalms 139:7-10; Matthew 28:20). He can, however, allow people to not recognize his presence for a time to develop dependence on him. The Bible describes God revealing himself in different ways and in greater and lesser degrees throughout people's lives. Jesus appeared in bodily form to the Apostle Paul (Acts 9; 1 Corinthians 9:1). At other times, he spoke through visions (Acts 16:9). Paul also had to rely on wisdom to make decisions (Acts 20:3). Likewise, Abraham saw God in human form (Genesis 18:1-15), but he also relied on visions and "the word of the Lord" (Genesis 15:1-5). Though, one day, God's children will see him face to face (1 Corinthians 13:12), faith and dependence are essential in this lifetime. For those who are righteous, the requirement of faith is not a punishment but a blessed way of life for "the righteous will live by faith" (Galatians 3:11).

14 Little child receiving his first pet: This was one place in particular where it was difficult to describe in words the emotions I was feeling. One would not typically be elated simply over receiving a bush. However, the satisfaction and the overwhelming feelings of being entrusted with responsibility were immense.

15 His training was so intimate: God is able to interact with every person in the world at the same time without detracting from the one-on-one intimacy experienced between him and each individual who is engaging him.

Chapter 6
Filled Up, Sent Out

16 Focus on those in the middle: Jesus often did this in his ministry. There was the occasional time when he accepted the invitation to a Pharisee's house or engaged in brief debate, but his main focus in a crowd was the common people who were still yet to fully formulate their view of him.

17 Felt guilty if they did not frequent the building: Guilt, mere religious duty, or obsession with a building are not proper motivating factors for meeting together with other sons and daughters of the king. On the other hand, a natural desire of the king's children is to spend time with one another (as described in Chapter 5). Drawing closer to the king inevitably produces a love for his children, and "Whoever claims to love God yet hates a brother or sister is a liar" (1 John 4:20). Additionally, the Bible warns against "giving up meeting together, as some are in the habit of doing" (Hebrews 10:25).

18 Nic's curiosity for the new wisdom of the kingdom: Nic and his curiosity closely paralleled the biblical character Nicodemus described in John 3, 7, and 19.

Chapter 7
World Systems

19 **Diabolical machines:** This is not to suggest that all TVs and all TV programs are evil. This chapter does, however, suggest that the influence of TV is more subtle and more far-reaching than most realize.

20 **Precisely mimic what the instructors demonstrated:** A classic question goes something like "Does society influence art, or does art influence society?" In this case, the clear message is that TV has directly impacted society, specifically in the area of the sexual standards and norms by which people live.

21 **Sectors of Society:** Though I was not usually shown specific localities to which this book applied, this section was highlighted to me as primarily addressing American culture. However, some of the principles in this section still apply to other countries or are universal.

Chapter 8
Fire and Water

22 **Trivia questions about the king:** Knowledge and history are clearly not inherently wrong, but they should not be used as a substitute or an impediment to relationship.

23 **Standard palace procedure:** The example set in the beginning stages of a journey is incredibly important.

24 **Pondered for many years:** Throughout the story, I would occasionally see myself in the future looking back at current events. This was one of those times.

Chapter 9
Setting Out to Fight

25 Everyone is either for or against the king: Jesus echoed a similar sentiment in Mark 9:40 saying, "Whoever is not against us is for us."

Chapter 10
The Old West

26 Set out straight for the palace: This and previous examples do not suggest that decisions for life transformation are always instant. In John 4:35-38, Jesus said that the harvest was "ripe" and then also indicated that seeing the opportunities in the harvest required seeing from the proper perspective. Forcing an issue before someone is ready is a mistake, but equally harmful is unnecessarily delaying someone who is ready to follow the king.

27 I was not the only one... I was the only one: This is a play on words. The woman's partner was saying that there were many others with similar homosexual desires. The king was using "the only one" to portray his unique and personal love for the woman.

28 Because of this, he loves me: God does not love people simply because they are different from other human beings, but he does take great pleasure in the unique design of each individual.

Chapter 11
Ebony

29 Struck them with blindness: Walking in poor character or moral compromise does not always immediately produce a decrease in power, giftedness, or ability. Because of this, success and immediate results are not always healthy indicators of moral rectitude or integrity.

30 **Where was this coming from?:** Several times in this chapter, I experienced thoughts and actions that I would not personally think or do. This was one of the main indicators that this entire story was not just for my own personal encouragement and understanding. From the beginning, this story and included messages were designed to be for an audience beyond just me.

31 **Follow them because of past victories:** As I listened to the king, he seemed to imply that my pride in previous accomplishments and my feelings of invincibility paralleled King David's mindset in 2 Samuel 11. While Scripture does not directly state that David fell into grievous sin because of arrogance, the Prophet Nathan's parabolic rebuke in 2 Samuel 12 insinuates that David thought he could do whatever he wanted.

32 **Forget everything I had done for the king:** This does not involve wiping one's memories clean. However, while we do build trust with others through a proven track record of walking with the Lord, we should never expect others to trust us solely based on our past accomplishments.

Chapter 12
Asia

33 **You would accomplish very little:** Jonah is one example of this in the Bible. In the midst of his rebellion against God, he still was able to testify of the power and justice of God to those on the ship to Tarshish. Yet, clearly, the level of impact and transformed lives were greater when Jonah did what God told him to do, preaching to the people of Nineveh.

34 **Grandmothers and mothers cases against their boys:** I'm not sure why there were only female parents and grandparents and

only male teenagers. But, this microcosm of relationships serves as an example for other relationships within the Asian cultural community.

35 **Road to sonship remains free:** Our invitation to sonship to God obviously cost Jesus a great price—his beating, death, and resurrection. Furthermore, Jesus said that anyone who followed him must give up everything for him (Matthew 10:35-39). Still, God's invitation is for all to come to him at no cost of works or material offerings (Isaiah 55:1).

36 **Didn't care one bit:** Again, this chapter along with others does not intend to suggest that all problems will be instantly solved if we step in to help. Instead, this story portrays a prototype of what is possible when reconciliation between generations occurs.

Chapter 13
Women

37 **Michael:** The name Michael means "Who is like God?" It is a rhetorical question implying that no one is comparable to God. I don't know if the woman calling me by my middle name instead of my first name, Jonathan, is significant or not.

38 **Address this age-old dilemma:** Having experience in a particular situation is often helpful. However, personally knowing the king and his ways is even more valuable than life experience.

39 **How they saw their women:** Here, "their women" is not used in a possessive or pejorative sense. Although this chapter is primarily about dating and marital relationships, it speaks to the larger issue of male-female interactions as a whole. "Women" is used here, as opposed to "wives," so as not to reduce the scope of this dialogue to only husbands and wives.

Chapter 14
Vanity Mirrors

40 It was truly difficult to watch: The point here is not that anyone who uses a mirror or makeup automatically becomes unattractive on the inside. This section should be understood in the context of the overall message of the chapter.

41 When searching my heart met its limit, I would then ask the King: King David had similar interactions with God. He often confessed areas in which he clearly knew he had strayed from God. Yet, at other times, he was not aware of any infractions but was conscious of the possibility (or probability) of hidden guilt. In the latter case, he asked the Lord to search his heart and reveal to him any anxieties or offensive ways (Psalms 139:23-24).

42 Seen glimpses of this for years: Here, I am referring to a long period of time that I had experienced both in the world of the palace and in natural time. As mentioned in the foreword, this book is a series of visions that did not take place all at once. Numerous times, at the end of a vision/chapter, I would get a glimpse of how this entire experience would end—the King on a throne of both intimacy and judgment. This culminating event occurs in Chapter 16.

43 Lisa: The name Lisa is a derivative of the Hebrew name Elizabeth meaning "Oath of God" or "God is satisfaction." The latter definition may be meaningful in this instance. Or Lisa may simply be a common female name used to represent many women.

Chapter 15
The Last Battle

44 King dancing through the streets: The king's dancing resembled King David's celebration in 2 Samuel 6.

45 **Many battles have been fought:** Warfare in the kingdom is often far different than earthly battles between opposing armies. The Apostle Paul said, "We do not wage war as the world does. The weapons we fight with are not the weapons of the world" (2 Corinthians 10:3-4). He continues by explaining that his battles are against false arguments and knowledge that opposes God. Paul also affirmed, "Our struggle is not against flesh and blood" but "against the spiritual forces of evil" (Ephesians 6:12). In the kingdom, wicked people are not the ultimate enemy.

46 **All the battles have already been fought:** This is not to suggest that no future events will happen on a global scale. But it is possible to devote so much focus to attempting to predict the future of the world that one misses his or her own personal calling and mission.

47 **All the battles have been won:** In the kingdom, victories often appear to be defeats. The Bible describes a group of people whose method of triumph is laying down their lives (Revelation 12:11). However, one day, every enemy of the king will be defeated and every battle will be won.

48 **Cruel to rejoice in their defeat:** Martyrs are one example in the Bible of those who are portrayed as being full of mercy yet also desiring justice. In Acts 7:51-52, Stephen tells a crowd, "You stiff-necked people!... Was there ever a prophet your ancestors did not persecute?" Yet, moments later, he prayed, "Lord, do not hold this sin against them" (Acts 7:60). In Revelation 6:10, a group of righteous martyrs in heaven cry out, "How long, Sovereign Lord, holy and true, until you judge the inhabitants of the earth and avenge our blood?" Jesus Christ also demonstrated both mercy and justice. On the cross, he prayed, "Father, forgive them, for they do not know what they are doing" (Luke 23:34). Later, Revelation 19:15 describes Christ, saying, "Coming out of his mouth is a sharp sword with which to strike down

the nations." The verse also states that he "treads the winepress of the fury of the wrath of God Almighty."

49 Release his son early for good behavior: The principle lesson in this section is not length of punishment but the nature of true justice. The topic of length of punishment is covered in the next chapter.

Chapter 16
The Final Palace Call

50 Seen this consummation for many years: See Endnote 39.

51 Grew to hate me more and more: Genesis describes people before the Great Flood as having far longer life expectancies. In that time, however, the longer people lived, the more wicked they became. Genesis 6:5 describes the situation, "Every inclination of the thoughts of the human heart was only evil all the time." Unlike fine wine, people did not become better with age.

52 Their torment would be far worse: Jesus taught that salvation is based on believing or not believing in him (John 3:16-18). However, judgment is based on what one has done (Revelation 20:13). Thus, individual punishments in hell will differ just as individual rewards in heaven will vary based on actions done in this lifetime. Had God allowed the wicked to live longer, they would have only stored up more future judgment for themselves. In contrast, God does not want the righteous to have to wait forever to receive their just reward and eternal inheritance. He is merciful to limit the years on earth of both the wicked and the righteous.

53 It is in casting them out, that I bring you in: God spoke a similar principle to Moses involving the Israelites and Egyptians, saying, "When I struck down all the firstborn in Egypt, I set apart for myself every firstborn in Israel, whether human or animal. They are to be mine. I am the Lord" (Numbers 3:13). God's love for his children is not the only reason for the existence of a place of torment, but it is an important reason that is often overlooked.

ABOUT THE AUTHOR

Jonathan Seiver has loved the nations and people groups of the world from a young age. Beginning with a high school ministry trip to Jordan and Israel, he has served and ministered across Asia, the Middle East, Africa, South America, Central America, and North America. There are few things he loves more than telling people the good news of Jesus Christ for the first time, especially in their native language. He currently speaks English, Spanish, Portuguese, and Chinese.

Jonathan also loves meditating on and teaching God's Word, the Bible. He earned a bachelor's degree in Biblical Studies and a three-year ministry degree, while serving two churches as a youth pastor. After Ministry school, he returned to teach Old and New Testament to the school's first year students. He hopes to continue his theological education in the future. However, beyond formal studies, Jonathan considers the lessons learned in his personal time with the Lord to be more transformative than any classroom lecture. Each one of the visions documented in *The Palace* was birthed out of deeply personal private times with the Lord. The two main themes of this book reflect Jonathan's heart: God is worth giving up everything for and he is a good Father, a King who wants sons and daughters.

Jonathan has spent the majority of his life in the suburbs of Chicago, Illinois. He would love to hear from you at seivermedia@gmail.com.

Made in the USA
Charleston, SC
08 December 2015